In the Name of
EFFICIENCY

IN THE NAME OF
EFFICIENCY

Management Theory and
Shopfloor Practice in
Data-Processing Work

JOAN M. GREENBAUM

TEMPLE UNIVERSITY PRESS
Philadelphia

HD
6976
.D372
U53

Library of Congress Cataloging in Publication Data

Greenbaum, Joan M., 1942–
In the name of efficiency.

Bibliography: p.
Includes index.
1. Electronic data processing personnel—United
States. 2. Industrial sociology. 3. Division of
labor. 4. Labor productivity—United States.
5. Electronic data processing departments—United
States—Management. I. Title.
HD6976.D372U53   658'.05'4   79-12213
ISBN 0-87722-151-0

Temple University Press, Philadelphia 19122
© 1979 by Temple University. All rights reserved
Published 1979
Printed in the United States of America

To Harriet Held Greenbaum

CONTENTS

vii

Acknowledgments

As I write this I am nearing my fifteenth anniversary in the computer field. Like many of the people with whom I worked during much of this time I felt that what was happening to me on the job was personal. In other words, when I liked my work less, some failing within me was responsible. It took me a while to realize that such "personal" experiences were happening to everyone—that changes within the occupation were in fact taking place. I decided to look at the changes occurring within the data-processing workplace, and this book is the result.

Unraveling what was done "in the name of efficiency" was long, arduous, and often quite lonely. The reinforcement I received from people during my investigation reaffirmed my belief in collective work activities, and I can honestly say that an important part of my learning process was in the exchange of ideas and the emotional support I received.

This study was first presented as a dissertation for Union Graduate School of the Union for Experimenting Colleges and Universities. The Institute for Policy Studies in Washington, D.C., provided tuition assistance, for which I am grateful.

I would like to thank my primary thesis advisers—Jeremy Brecher, David Gordon, and Len Rodberg—for their ideas and the manner in which they presented them. I believe that the way criticism is offered is as important as the ideas exchanged. We all learned how to give criticism a little better and I am pleased that we had the opportunity to grow in this way.

The project was conceived within the supportive environment of a women's study group begun in the economics department of the Graduate Faculty of the New School for Social Research. The study group helped me grapple with theoretical problems and gave me the strength and conviction to do the work. I have a very special feeling for the women in that group, notably Constance Blake, Janis Barry, Penny Ciancanelli, and Nadine Felton, because their method of throwing ideas around was so dynamic it literally propelled me to work.

I also had the opportunity to participate in a three-year series of workshops and discussions with the Work Relations Group. This group, concerned basically with study of the nature of work and action on it, was instrumental in helping me formulate many ideas. It gave me the chance to share my work experiences and compare and analyze them with others in other occupations. In particular, I would like to thank Stan Weir, who encouraged me to do something about my thoughts.

In addition, I am grateful to Marty de Kadt, who forcefully got me started by telling me to go "do it," and Sherry Gorelick, who stopped me from making endless corrections. Their support was invaluable, for, as anyone who has ever attempted a study knows, the beginning and the end are the most difficult parts. In a similar vein, Michael Baker, Sally Hillsman Baker, Dave Kotelchuck, Ronda Kotelchuck, Phil Kraft, and Bill Tabb were instrumental in helping me sort out the arguments made "in the name of efficiency." Various members of the Union for Radical Political Economics also helped discuss and criticize issues presented here—their strong sense of humor made the process more enjoyable.

It is traditional to close the acknowledgments by mentioning the people "without whom this would not have been possible." I have finally come to understand the meaning of the phrase. Laird Cummings not only helped me develop ideas and build them into this study but also provided the kind of support that made this possible. He shouldered the burdens of childcare and household work and responsibilities along with editing, proofreading, and suggesting, for what seemed to be a never-ending period of time. I cannot say which type of assistance was more valuable. I think that it is significant that he provided emotional support, technical help, and family care with the same degree of interest and love. And I want to offer special thanks to Brian, Barbara Jill, Jesse, and Bart for their patience with a mother who was always "at the typewriter." In particular I want to thank Brian, who as the oldest had to take the greatest share in helping with family responsibilities.

My special thanks are offered to the dozens of workers and students in the data-processing field who gave their time to this project. André Schklowsky and Bob Weisburd were unusually helpful in pointing out things to look for. Although I cannot list all the others by name, I would like to say that each person contributed original and insightful ideas.

PART

I

History
and
Theory

CHAPTER

1

Introduction

Back in the 1960s I was a computer programmer. Like most of the 200,000 or so other programmers, I enjoyed the work—particularly its opportunities for diversity and challenge. Comparatively high-paying, computer programming offered high status because its skills were little understood and in great demand. By the early 1970s some of the craftlike characteristics of this work had begun to change. The changes, like most day-to-day happenings, appeared quite slowly. But as they began to increase in tempo, it gradually became apparent that work activities once controlled by data-processing workers were no longer in their control. In 1972, A. P. Ershov, an outside observer of the data-processing situation, had this to say about the changes:

> The volume of work to be done is increasing, and wages less so. The romantic aura surrounding this inscrutable occupation is, if it ever really existed, beginning to fade. . . .
>
> Even the claim of programmers to be a special breed of professional employee has come to be disputed. Still more significant, authority over the freewheeling brotherhood of programmers is slipping into the paws of administrators and managers—who try to

make the work of programmers planned, measurable, uniform and faceless.[1]

From the time of Adam Smith's lengthy discourse on the division of labor in *The Wealth of Nations*, management has almost religiously recited the principle that labor must be divided into discrete steps. Our society is the result of a two-hundred-year-old experiment in this principle. Everything we buy, from McDonald's hamburgers to automobiles, represents the activities of divided and fragmented labor. But management would not be able to coordinate these subdivided activities if each task had not been pre-planned and carefully defined.

The events of the seventies are not discontinuous with the past. They are not created solely by the economic crisis, but are rather the logical outgrowth of prior management movements toward worker efficiency. Since the turn of the century, when Frederick Taylor began "Scientific Management," there has been movement toward increased routinization and repetition at the expense of worker decision-making and variety of tasks. Taylor's Scientific Management sought to develop methods to motivate blue-collar workers while removing the craft nature of their work and replacing it with repetitive functions, paving the way toward assembly-line operations, for once the workers' tasks were isolated and timed, it was possible to routinize them as activities along a conveyor belt. This change in industrial work was successful for industry managers. It created a consistent and predictable level of productivity and helped control the workers. Although white-collar spectators were reluctant to see this trend toward routine work encroach on their jobs, encroach it did, as the number of white-collar jobs expanded.

Although some management theorists have scorned the idea that this principle could be applied to the "elite" in the computer field, the majority of management practitioners marched along toward work division, standardization, and simplification. From a management perspective, the reasons are obvious; work that is not carefully planned, simplified, and divided *cannot* be brought under management control.

In the late 1960s academics were hailing increases in education and automation as two indicators of the coming humanization of work. Economic theorists, such as those from the "human capital" school, argued that increased educational levels indicated that Americans were preparing themselves for better and more challenging jobs.[2] Automation theorists foresaw the day when computers would be able to perform most routine functions, freeing workers to take on jobs that promised more variety and opportunity for thought. Yet by 1970 Ivar Berg and Sherry Gorelick reported that Americans were already overeducated for the jobs they held.[3] Similarly, a 1973 Health, Education, and Welfare Department study concluded that "many workers at all occupational levels feel locked-in, their mobility blocked, the opportunity to grow lacking in their jobs, challenge missing from their tasks."[4]

In what began as a personal study, I set out to explore what was taking place in data-processing workshops and why it was happening. Many have said that the changes in the work process were just the results of the "normal" changes that occupations go through as they mature. And in the growing body of literature about occupations I did indeed find that data-processing work was not unique. Many jobs, from auto mechanics to making x-rays, had undergone similar changes, or were in the process of undergoing them. In each occupation, as knowledge and skill were removed from the workers, pride, motivation, and job satisfaction eroded. What was most noticeable about the changes in each occupation was that they were anything but "natural"; workers fought against these forms of change, and managers had a hard time implementing them.

My purpose is not to bemoan the lost days of craftlike activity, but rather to highlight the history of the changes so that workers affected by them can better grasp the implications. The reasons for changes in the workplace are not always the reasons that appear on the surface. I want to peel away some of the masking reasons in order to identify the *purpose* of the changes. As long as developments in the workplace are made to appear natural, or inevitable, it is more difficult for people to influence them.

Although this is a case history of data-processing work, it can be relevant to other workers. To both blue-collar and white-collar workers who view their own jobs as boring and repetitive, the computer field has represented a bright spot on the horizon. Data-processing workers, with their status and technological tools, were thought to be free from the reach of occupational degradation. Most students at the community college where I teach and many data-processing workers still believe this to be the case. And if data-processing workers, with their status and technical skills, are not beyond the grasp of efficiency changes, how much more painful must be the plight of other groups of workers. While these occupational changes are quite pervasive the way that work is now organized is not the only way that it can be.

Most occupational change is made in the name of efficiency. Efficiency has come to be a catchword of the twentieth century. Although it usually means more output for each unit of input, it is so overused that it has almost lost its meaning. Together with phrases like "human resources," "labor-management problems," "labor productivity," and "technological developments," it envelops the issue of occupational change in a fog of mystification. If work is to be divided for the sake of increased efficiency, why is it divided in such a way that workers know *less* about what they are doing? When the divided work is reorganized, why is it put back together in the shape of a rigid hierarchy, so that those at the bottom have little say about the way work is done? And within the hierarchy, why are bureaucratic rules imposed over individual and collective decision-making?

Generally, managers claim that division of labor and specialization are made necessary by the size and complexity of the modern business organization. Management-induced change is often presented under the rubric "technical necessity." This sequence of events with technological explanations is made to seem natural and inevitable. In addition, management has argued that particularly in data processing the shortage of available workers has necessitated increased routinization of work activities. And although they admit that some changes may result in the temporary removal of skill from some workers, they argue that the end result will be a general upgrading of the overall skill level. But these issues do not explain the drive for efficiency; rather they further bury its meaning in faulty assumptions and oversimplifications.

Management bases its concepts of efficiency on a set of rules and procedures that today are called "management science." Although its roots are in Frederick Taylor's Scientific Management, the newer "science" is more eclectic in nature—representing a sort of souped-up version of its predecessors. According to the literature of management science, labor is a resource much like any other business resource. As such, it is there to be used, recycled, made obsolete, measured, and controlled so that the results of this resource can be predicted and planned for. But the problem that management continually faces is that this resource does not respond as predictably as other units of input in a management model for efficiency. When management talks about boosting the efficiency of labor (people) it means more than simply increasing worker productivity—it also means controlling worker reactions. The second meaning often conflicts with the first and sometimes even dominates the actions of management.

In the data-processing field, for example, management has called for changes in the work process in order to increase labor productivity (output of labor). Over the last twenty years, and particularly during the last decade, these changes required increasing rules, standards, and management control, all of which were intended to increase the efficiency of data-processing labor. But today, even though most of the changes followed the theories prescribed by management science literature, data-processing management is still struggling to cope with what they call the "people problem." It has been estimated that the programming costs *per instruction* in constant dollars have climbed from $4.50 in 1959 to more than $8.00 in 1976.[5] If efficiency in the form of decreased costs was the objective, in management terms we can only ask "what went wrong."

Some management authors argue that increasing costs are the result of "poor" management. They claim that management is indeed a science that must be used precisely in order to gain desired effects. Others complain that the theories of management are not yet well developed and therefore the results are unpredictable. "Hard-line" managers blame the permissiveness of "soft-line" managers, whereas "soft-liners" argue that "hard-liners" dominate workers too severely. In the midst of the managers' controversy, one thing is quite clear: *regardless of the management style that brought about the change*, the results have all been in the direction of management exerting more control over the work process and the worker. If data-processing management has not yet achieved its primary objective of decreasing costs, it has nonetheless established itself successfully in the second objective—controlling workers.

Changes in the work process, then, are a fundamental form of management control. Harry Braverman describes these changes as the essence of Frederick Taylor's policies of Scientific Management: they are designed to remove workers' private knowledge about the labor process from the workers domain and place knowledge and control in management's repertoire.[6] Social scientists call this category of changes "work rationalization." They involve breaking down each task "into a large number of smaller and simpler steps."[7] In management jargon the term "rationalization" carries a positive value; it makes things appear to be more rational and therefore more sensible. But rationalization buries the fact that divided and specialized labor removes skills from worker control—a predicament few workers find sensible.

Changes that make work more "cut and dried" obviously have an effect on the worker. Our consciousness—the way we understand ourselves and our society, as well as the way we act within that society—is shaped by the power relations we are pressed into during the working day. When thought process, creativity, social interaction, and physical mobility are taken away and replaced by rules and regulations that make us feel powerless, it is not surprising that our consciousness becomes limited and limiting. Work changes aimed at removing the very soul of the worker must indeed have a profound effect on the way we think and act. One hundred years ago Karl Marx commented that our social existence determines our consciousness.[8] Today it is clear that the social existence of the work culture still shapes our consciousness.

I found that the data-processing worker reacted on two quite different levels to the events shaping his or her job. One part of the individual seemed to accept management arguments for efficiency, grudgingly "admitting" that rules and standards are necessary for increased productivity and a more "rational" work environment. But another part reacted against most forms of change, causing management to shift tactics continually and adjust the work process to workers' preferences. Both "consciousness," so to speak, existed side by side in each person: the one that had been taught to follow rules and adapt to change and the one that felt that change was not in her or his own best interest and, in fact, wasn't rational. Richard Sennett and Jonathan Cobb describe similar conflicts faced by blue-collar workers:

> The arrangement of consciousness which puts competence "out there" gives a person boundaries within which he can feel freely and without a sense of responsibility for his social position. Dividing the self defends against the pain a person would otherwise feel, if he had to submit the whole of himself to a society which makes his position a vulnerable and anxiety-laden one.[9]

When workers talk of increased efficiency, the conversation is usually about producing better products and having more control over the way they make those products. Data-processing workers are no exception. Their suggestions for improving work procedures argue for less division of labor and more control over the quality of their labor. Maintaining a sense of dual consciousness is a painful process. Management science compels them to accept the way things are as the natural order, but their instincts and feelings rebel.

The changes that have been made in the name of efficiency are too widespread to be ignored and too entrenched to go away. They are not an accident of history; they are rather a reflection of both the economic and the social relations of the society. The division and organization of work represent a set of social relations that express the power relations in advanced capitalist society. Many management authors have argued that the particular form of these changes has not been successful because the very function of stripping knowledge and power from workers has caused workers to react "unproductively." Some have urged job enrichment and work humanization as counterbalancing forces. Yet their arguments are lost voices in the rising tide of job degradation and deskilling. The history of change within an occupation is also the history of a set of social relations.

In order to understand more clearly the purpose of management-induced change, I found it necessary to study both management literature and the consciousness of data-processing workers, tracing here the way management theory has shaped worker actions and, conversely, the way worker consciousness has affected the theories of management. I began by reading trade journals and the proceedings of data-processing society conferences; I found that, although they had the authoritative sound of written history, they did not capture the changes actually taking place on the shopfloor. Computer workers are quick to point out that the techniques presented in the management literature do not relate to what is happening to them on the job. I then focused on the differences between management theory and shopfloor practice by conducting numerous in-depth interviews with data-processing "old-timers" (in this field that means workers who have been around for ten years or longer!) as well as interviews with newer workers.[10]

Because the nature of data-processing work is so broad I limited myself to an investigation of commercial data-processing jobs; that is, to jobs of those workers involved in writing and running programs that process data for business organizations. Essentially, these data-processing workers are record-keepers, for they are the workers who maintain the electronic records that keep track of commercial transactions. This study is primarily about computer programmers and computer operators who work in medium to large corporations, because it is the jobs of these workers that have undergone the most noticeable changes. Within this category I have focused more on programmers than on operators, both because the nature of programming work has changed more markedly and because the amount of data available on computer operators is comparatively small. Until now, little has been written about the men and women who operate the computer equipment.[11]

Throughout, I try to contrast management arguments for efficiency in the work process with worker perceptions of the changes that have taken place. Part One traces the historical and theoretical developments within the field, first outlining the changes in data-processing occupations and then summarizing the history of computer technology and use. The intent is to dispel quickly the myth that changes in data-processing jobs are primarily caused by technological change. Whereas most data-processing workers know that technology itself is a product of people, it is important to trace the history in order to lay the foundation on which a more complete and interactive history of occupational change can be built. Part I also presents the management theories that have had an influence on change in the workplace. The developing theme is one of management theory as a set of principles that define the social relations within a society. It shows management theory as an *ideology of both economic and social control.* The major management theories that define and describe management science are outlined, and the growing body of radical theory which looks at the same events quite differently, is high-

lighted. In the drive for efficiency management employs
four types of strategies to mold worker activity. These
strategies include the need for management control over the
labor process, worker behavior, management organization,
and technology.

Part II describes the practice of these four strategies in the
data-processing field. What emerges here is a view of how
worker actions influence management practice. We see that
although management ideology is pervasive, data-
processing workers attempt to mold a shopfloor culture of
their own. We also see what happens when management
tries to implement its theoretical principles. The social
organization of data-processing work is examined, pre-
senting in detail the actions of management and reactions of
workers, describing the social customs and relations of the
workplace that help data-processing workers cope with an
attempt to change the existing power relations. The social
relations of the workplace are more than a set of neutral
bureaucratic principles. Efficiency and the management
strategies used to implement it are potentially explosive.
Data-processing workers may not perceive that they can do
much about it, but their actions on the shopfloor indicate
that they can go far toward redefining the way their work
lives are organized.

CHAPTER

2

History

Changes in an Occupation

Discussion about business cycles is as commonplace in the computer field as it is in any other. Clearly, the computer industry has gone through a number of distinct periods, reflecting changes in the cost and type of computer applications. But in examining these periods we must not lose sight of the larger trends, or tendencies, that have occurred over the length of the computer age. They all point in one direction: they show the particular features of an occupation that has been transformed from worker-regulated processes to management-controlled tasks.

The generally acknowledged start of the computer age is in the early 1950s.[1] The first business computers were used for purely repetitive clerical functions that previously had been done by electronic accounting machines. These machines, often seen as the predecessor to the modern computer, were based on electromechanical devices for processing keypunched cards. They evolved from keypunch-card procedures developed by Herman Hollerith for the Bureau of the Census in 1890. Large banks, insurance firms, and similar companies that had already established the clerical procedures for card systems were able to change over to the faster, but similar, computer systems by the second half of the 1950s. Since IBM had 90 per cent of the keypunch-card tabulating business, they were able to take a lead in the computer manufacturing business.[2]

Computers were applied only to those situations where the work process was already divided and rationalized. Accounting and payroll systems, for example, were prime targets for early computer applications because they required little or no change in the established work practices.[3] There was only one technical distinction between the first computers and their tabulating ancestors: the tabulating machines had to be wired each time an operation was to be performed, whereas the computers could be programmed with a series of instructions that could be stored for later use. But this distinction, coupled with the fact that computers were used *in addition* to existing tabulating equipment, created the demand for a large number of new workers.

By 1955, the industry urgently needed skilled people to operate, repair, and program the burgeoning computer applications. The workers who had previously operated the tabulating machines could fill this demand only partially. Business was expanding rapidly; the dollar volume of banking transactions doubled during the decade.[4] Insurance transactions expanded similarly.[5] As Alan Westin and Michael Baker point out, transaction volumes increased heavily between 1940 and 1955, lending credence to managers' claims to "file automation as an absolute necessity to cope with the tremendous increase in transactions."[6] IBM saw this period as one in which large firms were so burdened with increasing data-handling problems that they ignored cost considerations. A chief executive of the company described the period this way:

> At the dawn of the electronic data processing era, pioneer users of EDPM (insurance companies, large banks, Federal Government, airframe and defense industries), in the main, were not motivated by displaceable cost considerations. Sheer transaction

volume (or complexity of computational requirements) were such that the punched card technology
was inadequate regardless of quantity utilized.[7]

Lacking a large enough pool of trained labor-power,
computer manufacturers and companies using computers
began to lure people away from the sciences, often offer-
ing unlimited flexibility in their work as well as comparatively high wages. Programmers, in particular, were like
virtuosos in high demand, who could jump from job to job,
being granted demands to match their expectations. Almost
all were quite young, and they sought independence and
creativity in a field that promised status as well as high pay.[8]
Most computer workers were employed either by government contractors for aerospace and defense work or by
computer manufacturing firms. Only the largest computer
users (companies that use computers) like banks and insurance companies, for example, hired their own data-
processing workers.

Pirating skilled labor from other fields paid off for the
industry until the widespread use of computers began to
cause other pressures. By 1962, 10,000 to 12,000 computers
had been installed, with about 150,000 workers employed in
their manufacture, programming, operation, and maintenance.[9] At the time that workers were enjoying the effects
of a seller's market for their labor-power, management
journals and marketing literature were beginning to call for
standardization of job descriptions and routinization of
data-processing tasks. High on the management list of
reforms was an effort to stop the costly effects of personnel
turnover, created by workers jumping to more highly paid
data-processing jobs. Certainly, the 50 per cent growth in
computer workers' salaries during the 1958–1962 period
intensified the corporate drive to cut costs.[10] During the
early 1960s corporate management began to expect more
from computer applications. Early computer centers had
generally been charged to "research and development," but
by 1963 they were expected to show a "return on investment."[11] In addition, during the experimental decade of the

fifties, computer manufacturers had carried most computer software (programming) costs in an effort to gain new customers. Now the burden of labor costs was shifting to computer users, who were expected to design and implement their own applications. The need for middle and lower management to control the undisciplined, job-hopping work force, combined with the pressures from upper management to account for their growing expenditures, greatly hastened the death of craftlike worker activity.

The 1960s was a period of tightening the reins on the data-processing work force. Management stepped up its drive for "efficiency" and what it saw to be its necessary corequisite— division of labor and rationalized rules. The independent computer labor force with its concentration and interchange of skills among workers was clearly a threat to management. Both corporate and data-processing management cried out for procedures to control more closely the actions and costs of data-processing workers. Dick Brandon, an influential industry consultant, for example, argued that the industry had reached "economic maturity" without developing proper working methods, procedures, and disciplines. He called for tighter management controls, formal standards, and performance measurements, while decrying the "loss of management control" over data-processing functions.[12]

By 1965, when IBM began to install the general-purpose System 360, management demands for controllable data-processing labor were intensified. The new systems, which promised greatly increased speeds and storage capacity over the existing computers, supported the demands of computer-user management for greater worker productivity.[13] Those of us in the field at the time of the introduction of the System 360 tend to remember it well, for almost overnight a firm division of labor occurred, not by chance as it seemed to us then, but by clear design. Although computer work had been divided by task in the 1950s, many activities had overlapped a good deal. In particular, computer programmers and operators would meet in the computer room, which, like a social hall, offered the opportunity to exchange techniques and ideas. The installation of the System 360 provided management with reasons to change this. One of the first rulings to be enforced was a prohibition against programmers entering the computer room, thus isolating the two categories of labor and cutting off exchange of functions and rigidifying job classifications. From a financial point of view, corporate management saw the 360 as an increase in capital expenditure, requiring tighter controls and security. Thus, to them, the separation of operators and programmers was a necessary step in protecting their investment. Shopfloor managers were also quick to respond to the need to divide the work force in order to transfer some technical skill and control from the workers into their own domain.

In his excellent book, Philip Kraft describes the changes in the nature of programming tasks: "The transformation of programming is not the result of technological imperatives inherent in the logic of programming or computing. Programming has changed because managers, concerned about profits, have set about systematically and carefully to change it."[14] Computer programmers, who write the instructions (software) that make the equipment (hardware) actually work, were increasingly subject to rules, standards, procedures, and performance objectives that codified and routinized their tasks.[15] Computer operators were similarly molded. Operators tend the machines and see to it that the data are processed according to schedule. In addition to having standards and rules, their jobs were codified to the point where individual tasks became so routine that they were assumed by the computer system. Initially, for example, operators had to control the actions that started or stopped each step in the processing of an application. Improvements in computer software gradually incorporated these functions into automatic commands in the computer's operating or monitoring system.

It was during this period, when skills were removed from both operations and programming jobs, that the schools were beginning to turn out skilled computer workers. Universities were only too glad to respond to management pleas for more standardized programmers, and private institutes were quick to jump at the opportunity to make a profit training computer operators. Until the late 1960s computer manufacturers were the main source for training computer workers for few college or commercial programs existed. It was the joint demands for performance standards and an increased number of computer workers that pushed colleges to start computer science programs. Once begun, they churned out a large body of potentially disciplined future workers, giving management a larger pool of labor-power from which to choose.

During this process, as skill or craft work was abstracted from each task, programmers were encouraged to accept the myth of "professionalism," which kept them from organizing unions and seeing the changes for what they were. Indeed, strong evidence suggests that the impetus for professionalism has come from management and not from the workers themselves. Trade journals and computer associations, both overwhelmingly management organs, have strongly pushed the idea.[16] It seems likely that programmers, feeling the tide of job degradation, only too gladly clung to the belief that they were professional. Operators, lacking the "professional" designation, hung on to the status that came with working in an expensive "machine room."

But some of the glamor was removed in the early 1970s. In 1971, the Department of Labor decided that programmers were not professional employees and therefore were eligible for overtime pay. A federal judge upheld this in a 1976 decision, stating that programmers were not executive, administrative, or professional employees: "Of interest is the fact that a programmer does not need the expertise of the designer, need not know the inner workings of the computer, and can do adequate work with only a general familiarity of its function and a grasp of computer language."[17] The Department of Labor bulletin *Computer Manpower Outlook* noted "That some employers consider on-the-job training sufficient except for the top jobs (systems and management work) in a computer operation. They argue that the greater availability of college graduates in recent years enables them to hire persons with higher educational levels than is really required for the work."[18]

The 1960s saw the tightening of controls and the economic crisis of the early 1970s put the brakes on the data-processing field. Huge computer manufacturing firms, such as RCA, GE, and Honeywell, merged or went out of the computer business. Many small software and consulting firms also closed their doors, leaving computer workers for the first time in the midst of a declining job market. In 1972, an article in *Business Automation* commented: "Remember the people problem? It was a prime topic of conversation through the 1960's, but seemed to fade away in the past year or so. The job-hopping programmer or systems analyst will continue to be a rarity."[19] They characterized the data-processing labor market as one in which (1) personnel costs were stabilizing, (2) turnover was slackening, and (3) supply was approaching demand.[20]

Indeed, programmers' salaries began to reflect these trends. Breaking a long-standing upward curve, the average starting salary for programmers stayed at $8,500 between 1970 and 1972.[21] In 1975, a private survey found that programmers' salaries in large installations had risen only 2 per cent over the previous year, and yet large installations usually accounted for higher salaries and growth rates.[22] Computer operators met the same fate. The 1975 survey noted that their salaries did not increase between 1974 and 1975, a fact attributed to the "greater influx of entry-level people."[23] Yet the Department of Labor in 1974 cited labor costs as the prime ingredient in changing computer jobs:

> Because costs of computer manpower are a major part of computer user costs, manufacturers have a strong incentive to reduce the manpower needed to use their equipment by incorporating functions that currently are being performed by computer personnel into the hardware [equipment]. Also technological innovations that enable workers in other

occupations to interact directly with computers and thus eliminate costly data processing specialists are expected to be stressed.[24]

The emphasis on decreasing computer "manpower" requirements has been a main theme in the second half of the 1970s. The economic crisis that produced the phenomenon of the unemployed programmer also produced some marked changes in the computer industry. Back in 1967, some observers had forecast the possible saturation of the computer market in the United States with the then existing hardware and software.[25] In fact this appears to have happened. By 1970, 51 per cent of IBM's revenues was coming from foreign operations. Both the characteristics of the declining computer market and the effects of the economic crisis had an influence on reducing computer manufacturing costs and prices. Computer manufacturers put a good deal of research and development into reducing the cost of the technology. They were aided by the federal government, which during the 1960s provided between 57 per cent and 63 per cent of *all* funds for research and development.[26] By the late 1970s computer hardware costs had declined significantly, opening up new computer markets.

In 1977, the *Wall Street Journal* had begun talking about the new "Burgeoning Computer Software Industry":

> The cost of computer power had come down so far that the butcher, the baker, and the candle stick maker can afford computers. Minicomputers, for instance, are available to virtually anyone. The creative uses of this new level of computers are endless—video games, and everything. And so this new technology has opened up varied thousands of jobs.[27]

The use of remote terminals means, in effect, that any desk within reach of a telephone can transmit data over phone lines to a distant computer. Retail stores have begun to use these services for up-to-the-minute inventory reports, as clerks key in information on each sale. Banks, insurance companies, credit-reporting firms, and supermarkets are all tapping this new potential. The introduction of automated supermarket checkout counters has broken new ground in mass computer use. The late seventies have been called the age of the "mini" and "micro" computer revolution.

The expansion of computer applications to previously untouched areas has, once again, increased the demand for computer workers and brought about a slight increase in salary levels. Between 1975 and 1976 overall data-processing salaries increased at the rate of 5.7 per cent, although most of the larger increases were in managerial jobs. More current statistics show that the 1976–1977 increases have slowed to about 5 per cent with no increases for programmer or operator entry-level positions.[28] Although these percentages represent an increase over the early 1970s, cost-of-living increases have eaten up most gains for programmers and operators. Taking into account a 43.4 per cent cumulative cost-of-living increase since 1971,[29] 1977 entry-level salaries show no improvement over the early years of the decade. In 1977, commercial applications programmers at the entry level had a national average salary of about $11,000,[30] although the range ran from about $8,000 for coding, or lower level positions, to $15,000 for computer science graduates. Computer operators' salaries at the entry level range from $8,000 to about $10,000.[31]

But the economic expansion of the computer industry in the late 1970s is not the same as previous computer booms. The standards and procedures instituted in the previous decade and the chilling effects of the crisis in the early seventies have left their mark on the labor process for computer workers. *Quantitatively* the computer field is again expanding, but *qualitatively* a difference is involved for the workers. Data-processing jobs today are much more highly specialized and carefully defined than they were one or two decades ago. The performance objectives begun in the 1960s, although not as successful as most managers would like, now play a role in allowing management to control the schedules and actions of data-processing workers. Today, data-processing work is divided among systems analysts, programmers, and operators. Within each of these categories is an increasing number of subdivisions that separate workers. Programmers, for example, are specialized according to the type of industry for which they may write programs, such as insurance, banking, or manufacturing, and within these groupings they are usually classified by the type of computer language they use to code the programs. Even systems analysts who design the applications now produce their specifications within a framework of narrowly defined job steps.

The results for data-processing workers are quite evident. Increasing specialization limits their potential job mobility, putting a cap on management "turnover" problems. Rationalization of work procedures—in the form of rules, regulations, and prespecified work practices—cuts into their control over their actions on the job. And the "fear of unemployment" that materialized for the first time in the crisis of the early seventies has had a disciplining impact on workers' behavior. Many workers, particularly those that survived the layoffs, are more willing to adhere to management regulations. These trends are not likely to disappear. For data-processing management, the central focus still remains development of mechanisms to control data-processing workers. The computer industry has grown from fifty computers in 1955 to more than 155,000 general-purpose installations in 1976.[32] The number of data-processing workers has grown to somewhere in the neighborhood of 500,000 operators, programmers, and systems analysts in the mid-seventies.[33] It is estimated that of the total cost of a computer system today, roughly 75 per cent is attributable to software (program development, maintenance, and operation).[34] In other words, the major portion of data-processing costs is directly related to labor.

Controlling related labor costs of data processing is a major management concern, particularly as the market for computer systems continues to expand. The amount spent on workers particularly upsets managers as computer equipment (hardware) costs continue to decline. It has been estimated, for example, that the cost/performance ratio for hardware has improved 200 times since 1955, whereas programmer productivity, the main factor behind software costs, has risen only 3 per cent each year.[35] Experts in the field see labor's share of total costs continuing to rise. In 1977 Dr. Richard Tanaka, then President of the International Federation of Information Processing Societies (IFIPS), warned that, by 1985, 90 per cent of data-processing costs would be workers' salaries.[36]

Since labor costs as a *percentage of total costs* are increasing, managers look for ways to decrease their dependence on workers. From management's perspective, the figures indicate that machines, namely computers, look more productive than human labor. Philip Kraft describes what managers set out to do about this: "Indeed, the principle was simple: if managers could not yet have machines which wrote programs, at least they could have programmers who worked like machines. Until human programmers were eliminated altogether, their work would be made as machine-like—that is, as simple and limited and routine— as possible."[37] Over the last twenty years worker tasks have increasingly been divided and decision-making functions been absorbed by management. Yet for both workers and managers in the data-processing field it is still not clear if these changes have indeed increased labor productivity and therefore enhanced efficiency.

Changes in Computers and Data Processing

Most workers and managers at the bottom of an organizational hierarchy see technology as something that controls their actions. The frightening fact is that technology does control actions, but only to the extent that it was *designed to do so*. "Technology" seems to be one of the most overworked words in the English language. Since it is blamed or praised for almost everything we do, it is hard to get a firm grasp on what it is and how it developed.

According to the dictionary technology represents "the sciences of the industrial arts"—that is, it involves the application of knowledge to industry. Clearly, it doesn't fall from the sky, or, as pretwentieth-century tales would have it, technology is not developed by independent craftsmen tinkering away in their basements. The image of isolated individuals stumbling on important innovative break-throughs may be pleasant to retain, but this image just isn't true any longer. As Richard Hall explains: "Technological change does not occur in a vacuum. The organization, while critically affected by technology itself, is also the 'gate-keeper' in terms of implementing technological change or redesign of occupations."[38] Indeed, the main focus of IBM's defense in the government's antitrust case is the argument that its size is a necessary precondition for the accumulation of capital on a large enough scale to support technological development.

Technology is developed by certain groups of people for use by other groups. Its creation and use is a social process in much the same way that the organization of labor is a social process. It reflects the social relations of industry. In doing so, technology is of course limited by the power relations of the society. Whether the technology takes the form of a machine (hardware) or a set of programs developed to make the machine work (software), its development and use are determined by the activities of people. David Noble, studying the factors that led to engineering technology at the turn of the century, has this to say about technology:

> While it may aptly be described as a composite of the accumulated scientific knowledge, technological skills, implements, logical habits, and material products of people, technology is always more than this, more than information, logic, things. *It is people themselves*, undertaking their various activities in particular social and historical contexts, with particular interests and aims.[39]

Computer technology is not the sole determining force behind job change, even though this oversimplification is a frequent argument in management literature. It excuses job degradation without stopping to explain the complexities of the issue. The capsule history provided here is intended to squelch the technological determinist arguments by showing the interrelations between the *use* of computers and the development of computer technology. Although readers in the data-processing field may already be familiar with this history, it is important to keep in mind the interactions among changes in computer technology, computer use, and data-processing job structures.

In a computer system the hardware is composed of a Central Processing Unit (CPU) and any combination of input/output (peripheral) devices attached to it. The Central Processing Unit has three parts that together allow information to be stored and processed (changed) temporarily according to sets of instructions.

Basically, it works like this: data transmitted from a separate input device are temporarily stored in a section of the CPU called the memory or primary storage unit; another section, called the control unit, acts as a traffic director in controlling and coordinating the flow of data; the third section, known as the arithmetic/logic unit, actually does the work of calculation and logical comparisons. Popular literature often portrays the memory unit as a kind of "super brain," but it really acts only as a sort of temporary scratch pad: a place to hold data for processing by the real workhorse—the arithmetic/logic unit. When it is necessary to save information for future processing, or whenever results are needed, instructions must be included to tell the processing unit to transmit information from the memory unit to an output device. Secondary storage devices like magnetic tapes or disks are used to record information that may be used over again. When a company processes its payroll, for example, the information about each employee is maintained on a secondary storage device and then "read in" when processing is necessary. When the data are input for processing, one record (an employee) is processed at a time in the Central Processing Unit, although the processing is so fast it may seem as though more is being done. [40]

The pre-commercial origins of modern computer history

are usually traced back to the years during World War II when government funding was applied to military problems. The ENIAC, Electronic Numerical Intergrator and Computer, was completed at the Moore School in Philadelphia in 1945. Designed and built under the direction of John Mauchly and John Eckert, the processor was developed to calculate ballistic trajectories. By today's standards it was rather primitive; it stood 10 feet high and more than 100 feet long, and it had in excess of 17,000 vacuum tubes. Programming consisted of tediously rewiring the circuitry each time a new formula was required.[41] In addition to the ENIAC, a group at Harvard had been working on development of a processor that could store programs or instructions. The result of this effort was an electromechanical device known as the MARK I.

In the late 1940s Eckert and Mauchly left the Moore School and established their own company, which developed the first stored program computer—the UNIVAC I. Lacking sufficient capital to get the project off the ground, they merged with Remington Rand in 1950 and the following year they delivered the first UNIVAC I to the Census Bureau. The use of a computer by the Census Bureau marked its potential for record-keeping and widespread business use. Although the hardware was based on vacuum tubes that were fairly unreliable, the fact that programs could be changed without rewiring (the stored program concept) made the UNIVAC I a versatile machine. Five additional UNIVACS were built for government agencies before General Electric became the first private company to install a computer in 1954.[42]

It is clear that during the early 1950s Remington Rand, the manufacturer of the UNIVAC, had a "jump on the market." IBM rejected an offer to acquire the rights to this machine "because it felt that the greatest market potential for computers was in scientific rather than business applications."[43] The clamor for commercial computers—coupled with the developments of mass production techniques in computer manufacturing during 1954–1956—seems to have convinced IBM of the error of its ways. "By making the most of Sperry Rand's mistakes,"[44] IBM avoided becoming a brief footnote in history. In 1955, it overtook Rand for the computer manufacturing lead. By 1957, it had 78.5 per cent of the computer market.[45]

IBM entered the computer age with 90 per cent of the punched card tabulating business.[46] In 1956, IBM introduced the Model 650 computer, which became an instant success because it offered their tabulating-card customers an easy transition to computer use: since the 650 had a card-reading input device, it allowed IBM's large customer base to continue using their existing punched card-oriented systems. In the same year IBM brought out its first "family" of vacuum tube computers—the 702, 704, and 705.[47] This gave the company a wider product line than UNIVAC and solidly entrenched IBM in the computer business.

The vacuum tube machines were known as the "first generation" of computers. Like the first ENIAC, they were quite large and required constant maintenance because tubes continually had to be replaced. In 1958, UNIVAC started what came to be known as the "second generation" of computers when it brought out the UNIVAC Solid State 80, which relied on transistors. RCA followed the transistor revolution, to be joined belatedly by IBM in 1959, when it began its 7090 series. Transistors had first been developed in 1948 at Bell Telephone laboratories and were used in the early 1950s for military equipment, but they were considered too expensive at the time for commercial application. Both government and business research and development efforts were applied to the problem of mass-producing transistors. By the late 1950s the cost of producing transistors was drastically reduced. Most observers agree that the second generation represented a technological break with the first, because the advantages of transistors in size, speed, and reliability were important in gaining general business recognition for computer potential.

It was during this period that IBM introduced the 1401 model, which caught on even faster than the 650. Like its predecessor, the 1401 offered tabulating-card users the opportunity to process their existing card-oriented applications faster. The 1401 became the workhorse of business; by 1964, more than 7,000 models were in use.[48] It was a big success in those industries like banking and insurance where rapid growth had made it difficult to handle the increase in record-keeping. In 1964, Honeywell delivered its H-200, modeled after the 1401 and considered by some a "technically very superior machine." Its introduction forced IBM to upgrade the 1401 models and develop competitive new products.[49]

Business expansion and the success of early computers in addressing the problems of business forced the computer manufacturing industry to find cheaper and more reliable components for computer construction. The second computer generation, lasting roughly from 1959 to 1965, was brought to an end by the introduction of integrated circuit components in the IBM 360 "family" of machines. The integrated circuit added speed and reliability to computer potential, but its development did not cause as sharp a break with the past as did the transistor revolution. Integrated circuits, like transistors, had been around for a decade before they were applied to general use. They had originally been developed by Texas Instruments and Fairchild Semiconductor for military products. From the standpoint of computer users, the IBM 360 was important because it was designed to offer compatibility between scientific uses and business applications as well as the interchangeability of input/output devices with CPU models. Even more important was the promise of interchangeability of operating system and program language software. Computer users had been clamoring for such developments since the late fifties. Despite delays in delivering IBM 360 models and major problems with software development, the IBM 360 was accepted as a "general-purpose" computer for a wide range of business applications.

Computer manufacturing competitors tried to cut into IBM's lead, but the 360 cemented IBM's dominance. In 1964–1965, RCA presented its Spectra 70 series, which was of identical design but faster, cheaper, and made entirely of monolithic circuits. Its appearance forced IBM to "upgrade" its product line, but it failed to capture a foothold in the computer market. General Electric developed the 600 series, which offered new technology for time-sharing (many computer users sharing the same CPU at the same time). Like RCA's attempts, that of GE was unable to penetrate the market despite time-sharing, which was declared the "thing of the future" and widely demanded by business. General Electric's emphasis on time-sharing, however, forced IBM to alter its 360 hardware and software designs radically so that time-sharing could be added to IBM equipment.[50]

With expanding markets, computer manufacturers were able to concentrate on lowering manufacturing costs. Integrated circuits gave way to large-scale integration (LSI), and refinements in the manufacturing process resulted in increased speed and reliability along with rapidly decreasing prices. In 1965, a medium-sized IBM 360 cost between $700,000 and $800,000; by 1976, a comparable machine (although much faster) cost about $380,000. The same type of machine in 1953 would have cost about three million dollars. Expressed in terms of "memory capacity per dollar of rental," 1977 computers delivered about eighty times the capacity of the first-generation devices.[51]

Mass-production techniques now pack thousands of circuits onto silicon chips that are smaller than postage stamps. The miniaturization process, coupled with decreasing manufacturing costs, has enabled companies to develop minicomputers and microcomputers. These units have opened up new markets for computer manufacturers as smaller businesses now find computers within their price range.

Today, as the silicon chips become cheaper and more interchangeable, they offer management a strong inducement to replace software with hardware components. In other words, it is now possible to replace more of the human labor of programming and operations with inexpensive and reliable pieces of equipment.

The history of systems software development is perhaps

best characterized by its constant lag behind hardware developments. By the late 1950s corporate users' groups such as SHARE and GUIDE had organized to try to begin measuring throughput and looking for ways to improve it. The biggest complaint from corporate management was that having invested so much in capital equipment they wanted some way to see it put to constant, efficient use. Operating systems were the answer, but their development rested on the use of programmers to write the necessary programs. And program development, of course, relied on labor-intensive activities, which in the early days had not been taken from their craft roots.

First-generation equipment was characterized by its lack of systems software support. Each time a program had to be run the operator would have to load the program and essentially start up the hardware. Programs were written in binary machine language, a tedious and time-consuming undertaking. By the end of the 1950s program language translators such as FORTRAN were gaining acceptance as were rudimentary operating systems. These early batch-processing operating systems made it possible to "compile, assemble and load [translate and store] a program with test data in one trip to the machine room."[52] Today this procedure is of course assumed, but at the time it represented a tremendous improvement in both machine efficiency (increasing the throughput of the hardware) and programmer and operator efficiency (taking less labor time).

Second-generation hardware "came with" its own operating system and program language translators. These support programs were leased as a package with the hardware. They offered greater machine and labor efficiency but posed two major problems. The first was a technical dilemma—the support programs that helped the equipment perform better were themselves inefficient because they required too much memory space. The bigger and more useful the operating system, the less room there was for user programs! The second problem was one of compatibility. Each computer manufacturer, and in fact each computer model, had its own systems software. The IBM 1401 commercial model, for example, used operating systems and languages radically different from the scientific-based IBM 7090 series. This had advantages for the computer manufacturer because it virtually insured that customers would not switch products; their programs would not work on a competitor's machine or a different model. From the corporate user's perspective, differences between software packages created tremendous training costs, for corporations had to train their data-processing workers in the specifics of each machine and its associated software. Corporate users complained so bitterly that compatibility (standardization) became one of the chief design considerations behind IBM's third generation of hardware and software.

By 1965–1966, IBM was investing as much in software design as in hardware.[53] The operating systems allowed much greater throughput by making it possible to process more than one program at a time. Since third-generation hardware made memory space comparatively cheaper, it was possible to build machines with more capacity, diminishing the second-generation storage problem. But third-generation software lagged severely behind the introduction of the hardware. By 1967, two years after the installation of the first 360, corporate management was still complaining that the promised features of the software support had not been delivered. And programmers' and operators' complaints were even louder. "Bugs" in IBM's mammoth operating system were more common than smooth performance.[54] At the time, IBM kept promising users that the "next release" of the operating system would solve their problems. A decade later Frederick P. Brooks, Jr., the manager of the Operating System project, freely admitted its problems: "The product was late, it took more memory than planned, the costs were several times the estimate, and it did not perform very well until several releases after the first."[55] Brooks argues that the problems in software development stemmed from inadequate division of labor and control over the programmers. Now, after two decades of experimenting with the organization of programming labor, large-scale operating systems are able to

CHAPTER
3

Theory

Management Theory: From Scientific Management to Management Science

Despite the great changes in management methods and styles since the turn of the century, the objectives of management remain the same. They specify that the function of a firm is to grow, and that the growth process is dependent on the accumulation of capital. In order to provide the environment to foster such a growth process, management must effectively allocate the firm's resources.[1]

Management literature reflects and defines the courses of action that can be chosen by policy-makers in a firm. The literature plays an important role in telling us how top corporate managers *perceive* their environment and how these perceptions delimit their choice of solutions. The solutions management presents are clearly not the only possible ones, but they are the most likely choices based on management's definitions. Within the pages of management literature, for example, efficiency of all resources—both people and things—is determined by the ability of management to control, measure, and predict the outcome of the labor process.

The literature outlines the policies available to top management for guiding its planning process; but it does not necessarily specify the way decisions are carried out, nor does it describe what actually takes place in a firm. Management writings range from theoretical to specific "how-to" categories. Theoretical principles are often quoted and argued as the basis for defining problems and highlighting the range of solutions open to management planners. Despite repeated attempts to define management as a science, its theoretical writings do not represent a unified body of knowledge or a firm set of principles. Management "theory" is probably best described as a developing set of definitions and strategies. The wide range of theoretical styles reveals differences in perceptions of workplace reality and in the type of solutions espoused. On the most general level, the opposing views have been characterized as theory X and theory Y; theory X represents the school that places formal authority and coercion in the primary position, and theory Y emphasizes worker collaboration, motivation, and human relations.[2] Obviously, these characterizations represent a polarization of management attitudes, but they are helpful in pointing out the differences in management's perception of labor. All management theory views labor as a resource, like raw materials or energy, but the theories differ in their methods for increasing this resource's output and decreasing its cost. For management, the problem is simply this: most resources respond to definable and quantifiable management techniques for increasing output; labor does not.

Theory X proponents basically see labor as a resource constantly fighting for its goals at the expense of the firm's growth; therefore, coercion and authority are necessary to force this recalcitrant resource into line. Theory Y advocates also perceive a "problem" with labor's behavior within the firm, but they argue that workers are basically agreeable people who can be motivated to produce more for the firm. Both start from the same base in that they perceive that workers resist the conditions of labor, and both agree that this situation must be better controlled. Douglas McGregor, the originator of the "humanistic" theory Y, had this to say about management: "One of the major tasks of management is to organize human effort in the service of the economic objective of the enterprise. . . . Successful management depends—not alone, but significantly—upon the *ability to predict and control human behavior.*"[3]

Both theories are threads that have been woven into the fabric of current management styles. Starting with the Scientific Management school in the early part of the century, through the "human relations" movement beginning in the 1930s, and on into the synthesis of these ideas in the framework of management science after World War II, management theory can be traced. Management practice differs from theory, because it is closer to the scene of worker reaction and is therefore forced into making on-the-spot decisions, but even these decisions are defined within the framework provided by management theory.

The introduction of Scientific Management by Frederick Winslow Taylor in the early part of the century has been considered so significant that some have called it the "Second Industrial Revolution."[4] Most management textbooks date modern management theory from Taylor's writings. Taylor's Scientific Management addressed the problems of management control of the labor process as they related to the increased size of corporations in the beginning of the era of monopoly capital. His efforts were aimed at increasing the productivity of each department within an enterprise by compelling workers to intensify their labor. Intensification of labor was brought about by time-motion studies, in which outside experts observed the labor process and then set standards for increased productivity. Workers were offered financial incentives for increasing their output. Control over the *pace of work* and *definition of tasks* was taken from the worker and placed in the hands of management. Once the stopwatch was brought into the workplace it dominated workers' actions. Down to the level of body motion they were defined and standardized so that managers could enforce the intensified procedures.

In management literature Taylor is probably best known for this emphasis on separation between thought and action. The application of time-motion study to work activities was designed to abstract each of the "simplest elements" of each job in order to squeeze from these elements the parts that required knowledge and those that did not. By doing this, Taylor tried to show that management did not have to sit idly by while workers controlled the *pace* of their labor. His message was that management could regain control of the labor process by removing skill and knowledge from the workers' arena and incorporating it into management functions. The message was particularly attractive to management because industrial production was dominated in many areas by craft workers who did, in fact, have a degree of control over production based on their knowledge of the work process. Taylor's Scientific Management sought to break that control.[5]

Scientific Management not only represented a new approach to administration of workers, it also caused a change in the social system of work.[6] Within the social system of the workplace, power shifted from workers to managers. In the past, when workers had controlled their shopfloor activities, their knowledge of the work process gave them considerable leverage in dealing with management. Scientific Management pried that power loose. According to Peter F. Drucker, the basis of Scientific Management is "the organized study of work, the analysis of work into its simplest elements and the systematic improvement of worker's performance of each of these elements."[7]

Scientific Management did seem to result in increased output in most instances where it was at least partially applied, but the problems it created between labor and management were far-reaching. In a study of Taylorism at the Watertown Arsenal (1905–1915), Hugh Aitken found that the system succeeded in more than doubling the old rate of production, *but* its impact as a social system seriously affected continuation of that increased output. Worker unrest and reaction were so severe that the federal government outlawed Taylor's system from further application in government installations.[8] Douglas McGregor has argued that because Scientific Management alienated the worker, it was costly in terms of sabotage and the rise of union militancy.[9]

By the late 1930s labor had built a sufficiently strong base through the union movement to be felt in many industries. The Depression increased the tempo of labor unrest. Rather than continue the openly antagonistic policies of Taylorism, management theory began to embrace the concepts of the "human relations" school: "it was no accident that the Human Relations movement followed in the wake of scientific management, mopping up the human residue left behind by the mechanistic organization of the work process."[10] Although increased output remained the order of the day, human relations theorists attempted to control workers by getting them to adjust better to their environment. If necessary, even the reverse—adjusting the work environment to worker needs—was called for if it did not conflict with overall corporate objectives. Perhaps the best-known example of this approach was the work of George Elton Mayo in the study of the Hawthorne Works at Western Electric Company. In contrast to Scientific Management and its unrelenting emphasis on quantifiable efficiency, human relations theorists interjected the concept of worker morale. The Hawthorne studies remind managers that improved human relations will improve morale, which in turn will increase production.[11]

This school of thought brought the social sciences into the management camp, introducing many new approaches to the problem of increasing worker morale.[12] Today, the writings that grow out of this school are heavily loaded with phrases like "human factor engineering," "human asset accounting," and "controlling human resources";[13] expressions that reduce human beings to abstract concepts conforming to the vocabulary of efficiency. The language of human relations attempts to create quantifiable terms by lumping people and things together. Scientific Management failed to consider individuals and nonmonetary matters, and human relations theories represented a management-defined step to correct the imbalance, but this approach would not survive, intact, the business transformations following World War II.

In his study of management change Maarten de Kadt states that "the control of labor has been a process that management has had to learn and to enforce anew in each period of newly expanded production."[14] Just as reactions to Scientific Management and the problems of continued accumulation induced changes in management theory during the 1930s, the problems of expanded accumulation after World War II created a new set of management dilemmas.

The approach developed over the last thirty years has come to be known as "management science." It incorporates Taylor's principles of efficiency and Mayo's theories of motivation into a body of knowledge that seeks to maximize the efficiency of the organization as a whole while minimizing the problems of worker resistance. Included in this synthesis are the tools and techniques of measurement developed during the Second World War for allocating resources to the battlefronts. These techniques, such as PERT (Progress Evaluation in Real Time) and Operations Research (OR), together with methods of analysis called the "systems approach," have given management its "scientific" base. Merging the behavioral and mathematical approaches, and at the same time borrowing freely from earlier management theories, management science stands prepared to juggle the complex problems of expanded growth.[15]

The most fundamental departure from Scientific Management is the view of efficiency as *more than simple cost reduction.* Imbedded in management science is the recognition that trade-offs are necessary between controlling workers and increasing their output. The systems approach emphasizes that the efficiency of the whole (the firm) may be different from the efficiency of its individual parts (units or departments).[16] Whereas Taylor tried to optimize the productivity of each worker in each department, management science indicates that efficiency of some departments may need to be sacrificed for the benefit of the whole organization—simply stated: the whole is not necessarily the sum of its parts. This idea provided a breakthrough in management thinking, for it allowed planners to support staff departments that were not efficient in and of themselves but provided services that helped bolster efficiency in other units. Data-processing departments, as well as legal, financial, and engineering functions, fit within this framework. Drucker stresses that the "system" is a social one and must be considered in this light:

> In some cases the best way to strengthen the system may be to weaken a part—to make it less precise or less efficient. For what matters in a system is the performance of the whole. . . .
>
> That the enterprise is a social rather than a mechanical system makes the danger [of emphasizing individual efficiency] all the greater.[17]

This concept of a system allows management to trade efficiencies throughout the firm and also to bring the principles into play at the level of individual workers. Its base rests on Taylor's principles for dividing labor, but it gives management the option of dividing certain tasks and at the same time integrating others. Scientific Management attempted to *fragment the tasks of each worker*. Management science makes it possible to apply the "right" motivating and/or fragmenting techniques in individual situations. Hales, in a study of the two schools of thought, summarizes the comparison this way:

> Scientific Management attempted to split up work into fragments, externally regulated. Operations Research, by virtue of its systems methodology and statistical techniques, can attempt the *integration* of systems activities which have their own internal structure of regulation.[18]

Isolating decision-making activities also makes it possible to apply Taylor's division-of-labor schemes to mental tasks. Herbert Simon, one of the best-known theorists for management science, emphasizes that new concepts of decision-making are necessary to divide white-collar actions into discrete tasks. He outlines three basic types of decisions that take place within the firm and explains how each can be made more *routine* and therefore subject to management planning. Essentially, Simon applies the tools of observation and measurement used by Taylor to the nonroutine functions of the firm.[19] In addition, his techniques are fully supported by the mathematical and statistical tools of management science, which allow management to build "control systems" based on *prespecified decision-making rules*. Rationalizing decision-making power goes one step beyond Taylor's techniques for removing worker skill and knowledge, for it allows a total separation between thinking and doing.

The emphasis on quantitative measurement of everything from worker actions to decision-making practice is a central focus of the literature of management science. Because management theory advocates quantitative measurement so persistently, many management practitioners are caught in the bind of measuring so many aspects of their operations that they find themselves drowned in a sea of quantitative reports.[20] Despite the sins of excess committed in the name of measurement, it is emphasized because it enables managers to plan and predict the functioning of each part of the enterprise and its relationship to the whole. The label "science" justifies the measurement of all variables in the production process, certainly including the quantification of what management calls its "human resources."

Management science literature places great importance on management's ability to predict and control each corporate resource. C. West Churchman, for example, outlines the way the systems approach can be used to *define each step in the work process* in order to bring it within range of management control procedures.[21] Alfred Chandler focuses on organizational policy that is aimed at gaining consistency, control, and predictability for the firm within its market. His emphasis on consistency *extends* the simple function of cost reduction by utilizing procedures to make the firm respond flexibly to its environment.[22] And Douglas McGregor reminds us that "progress in any profession is associated with the ability to predict and control."[23]

At the most fundamental level, management theory addresses itself to the actions and behavior of workers. Central to the management of labor is the ability to carry out policies that increase the productivity of this resource. But increasing labor productivity is a complex issue, often plagued by problems that the literature calls the "unintended consequences" of management policy.[24] Terms such as "conflict," "resistance," "negative reactions," and "labor response" appear throughout management writings—but always with the warning that "good" management can control workers without such consequences.[25] Management science accepts the idea that workers may not always see policy in the "proper" light; worker resistance, therefore, can be expected, but ways to counter it also must be planned.

The ability both to increase labor productivity and to retard labor "unrest" demands the control and coordination of four essential variables: the work process, the behavior and discipline of workers, the shape of management organization, and the technology used in production.[26] Although this is no small feat for management, the parameters are made more complex by constant changes in market conditions and by the actions of workers. Every period of accumulation brings a reshuffling of the priorities and tactics involved in controlling these variables.

Labor process. Modern techniques for controlling steps in the work process date back to Taylor's efforts to make work procedures standardized and therefore more predictable. Changes in the process involve *observing*, *defining*, and *standardizing each action or task*. Clearly defined tasks make it easier for management to establish expectations about worker productivity. Scientific Management used time-motion studies to codify the work process. Within the framework of management science, those studies have been expanded to include operations research techniques for modeling and simulating change and the tools of systems analysis for defining the trade-offs between morale and efficiency.[27] Operations research provides the mathematical base for management to manipulate variables and create mathematical models for observing the consequences of change. Systems analysis provides the methodology for systematically isolating and analyzing current activities and planning for future action. Together, they set the parameters for the minimum and maximum limits of change that are realistic to anticipate.[28]

Worker behavior. Despite the mathematical tools available, the issue still remains whether or not management can create models of actions that accurately reflect worker rebellion. Failure to include variables that describe methods of worker reaction or failure to weigh such variables properly can severely affect the "solutions" provided by the model and ultimately the success of these solutions. Predicting worker behavior is quite different from planning the sequence of tasks in the work process.

The term "labor discipline" is central to management discussions of worker behavior. The more disciplined the worker is, the more likely he or she will be to adopt clearly defined work habits. Management texts outline strategies for selecting, educating, and motivating workers who demonstrate good work habits. McGregor's definitions of theories X and Y apply to the question of worker motivation. Authors that lean toward theory X remind managers that workers do not like work and should be coerced into accepting more productive behavior.[29] McGregor, and others of his persuasion, argue quite the opposite, maintaining that people want to enjoy work and actively seek ways to gain self-satisfaction from work activities. This more positive emphasis favors motivational strategies that involve the worker more.[30] Both theories, however, call for motivational schemes that include promotion ladders, behavioral "trait" rating (performance evaluation), and management control systems. These mechanisms, like the mathematical models of the work process, allow management to quantify factors concerning worker behavior.

Management organization. Management's ability to

shape the organizational structure of the firm is critical for control of effective decision-making.[31] The degree to which top management can issue policy that will be effectively enforced by middle management and put into operation by the supervisory level is the essence of organizational structure: the shape of the organization can determine whether or not policy will be carried out.

Control over information is a key objective of organizational strategy. In the early part of the century Henri Fayol established a set of administrative principles that, like Taylor's work, remain at the root of most policy today. Fayol's principles called for "unity of command," in order for information to flow down a chain of command in which each person could receive orders from only one supervisor.[32]

Since the Second World War, organizational structure has shifted from centralized to decentralized.[33] Reshaped, it now includes forms of matrix structure which combine characteristics of the earlier structures.[34] The literature of management science contains a wide range of arguments about the "best" form for organizations. Drucker, for example, argues that differences between industries are important in determining the necessary degree of centralization or decentralization. The differences may be based on the extent to which the industry is "knowledge-based" (dependent on technical processes) and on the amount of competition present.[35] Other factors, such as the similarities and differences between occupations, may influence the choice of organizational structure.[36] Regardless of the specific shape of the organization, management texts agree that hierarchical structure and "information control systems" are required to carry out administrative policy.

Technology. Last, and certainly not least, is the necessity for management to allow for changes in the technical base of production and in the design of the product itself. According to management theory, technological innovation is a *process*, which, like the labor process, must be controlled and predicted.[37] The extensive funding of research and development efforts, through both private and government sponsorship, attests to the importance of the need for careful planning of the technical process.[38]

Some authors see technology as a determining force—one that defines the types of jobs and characteristics of the organization. But management theory, in general, is quite explicit about the need to *plan for technological developments* that meet the objectives of the firm. Management policy sets the parameters of technological design. It calls for concentration on developments that will *decrease costs* (both labor and materials) *and at the same time create a predictable level of performance.* Workers and lower level managers feel trapped by technology, whereas management science formulates policies that shape its characteristics. Contrary to the popular view that technology shapes jobs, Drucker argues that the organization of work (which must be controlled by management) influences technology: "The aspect of work that has probably had the greatest impact on technology is the one we know the least about: the organization of work."[39]

By focusing on the coordination of these four variables, management science recognizes that labor management is far more complicated than the old "kick-in-the-pants" school. It offers no single unified body of theory that best describes the tactics to follow, but it does provide a framework, through mathematical models and behavioral science, to isolate, define, and predict labor productivity. In doing so, it represents an ideology for social control.

Indeed, Drucker's view of management is one in which "management . . . [is] the central social function in our society."[40] Viewing management as a "discipline" rather than a "science," he sees well-organized management as that function which not only coordinates the enterprise, but also controls the economy and allocates the social resources. For Drucker, efficient management is a critical *social* function, for its effectiveness can determine how well the goods and resources of a society are distributed. His notion of the mission of management certainly takes it a long way from the "invisible hand" of Adam Smith. His vision indicates that society can be coordinated and controlled through the theories and ideology of modern management. Smith's "invisible hand" becomes embodied in the highly visible actions of corporate management.[41]

Radical Theory: Labor Is More Than a Resource

The division of labor found in the workplace, with its fragmented jobs, overpowering technology, and rigid bureaucracy, is but one form of work organization. It is the form dictated by the goals of management science as it attempts to mold the social relations of the workplace. Behind the facade of managerial efficiency lies the power of managerial control over worker actions. Although most changes in the labor process are made to seem impersonal, they represent the exercise of managerial power over workplace control.

Radical theory examines the roots of the struggle to control the workplace and points to ways that work can be reorganized.[42] It looks at the way people try to enhance and upgrade their jobs rather than deskill them. It explores cooperative, collective work groups that arise in the midst of authoritarian, bureaucratic structures, and it emphasizes that fragmented jobs divide the self and weigh upon the consciousness of the individual. David M. Gordon distinguishes two forms of management efficiency: a "quantitative" one that management refers to when it looks for increased output; and a "qualitative" one that attempts to minimize workers' resistance by disciplining them to accept the current social relations.[43] An understanding of the second goal is necessary to demystify the things done in the name of efficiency.

The history of twentieth-century management theory is the history of increased quantifying, measuring, and predicting of "input" and "output" factors in the corporate productive equation. Managerial efficiency measures the ability to decrease the input of certain resources and/or increase the output, or results. The term "efficiency" for example, usually involves a whole string of variables: "Essentially, economizing means efficiency, least cost, greatest return, maximization, optimization and similar measures of judgment about the employment and mix of resources."[44] Management science, with its bag of quantitative tools, has had the greatest success with computing efficiency ratios for resources like raw materials, equipment, inventory, and other nonlabor "inputs." But labor continues to cause the biggest variance in calculating predictable statistics. The difference between labor's input and the output, or product, is marked and often erratic; sometimes it is not even quantifiable.

For radical theorists the distinction lies in Marx's differentiation between labor-power and labor. Labor-power is what the worker sells in the marketplace—it is the worker's *ability* to work. Labor, on the other hand, is the actual expenditure of physical and mental tasks *on the job*. In other words, management purchases labor-power, but what it gets, in the workplace is the amount of labor the worker wants to, or is forced to, deliver. The conversion of the purchased labor-power into actual labor is affected by the struggle between management and worker interests. Management theory seeks ways to extract more labor from the labor-power it has hired.[45] Labor, then, is not an "automatic" input. Within limits set by the firm, workers choose the way in which they use their own resources. Managerial complaints about worker productivity are really arguments for changing the limits management has established. The more the limits shift toward management priorities, the more management can predict the level of worker output, and thereby begin the process to limit its cost.

Management theory indirectly addresses this distinction by outlining strategies that trade outright quantifiable efficiency for morale and "environmental factors." The root of the issue is concern over labor productivity. Whereas management literature blandly describes this problem as one requiring increases in labor input without corresponding increases in labor cost, radical theory emphasizes the *power relations* that come into play. Workers do not willingly give up control over the direction and pace of work. To do so would be to give up whatever power they have over their job. Radical theory examines such transfer of power from workers to managers. It also looks at the reactions of workers and their methods for regaining control. According to radical theory, productivity is not the neutral term management theory paints it to be. Increases in productivity require shifts in control, which do not occur without a struggle.

Stephen Marglin, for example, looked at the shifting power relations in his historical study of the rise of the factory system. He concluded that the "success" of the factory system of labor organization was not solely based on its technical efficiency—it did not necessarily produce more in quantitative terms. Rather, he argues, the factory system allowed management to coordinate and thereby control workers under one roof, in essence providing an environment where work *discipline* and *control* could be enforced. The basis of this form of discipline is management's ability to control factors that affect labor productivity.[46] Marglin's conclusions about pretwentieth-century labor organization have been confirmed by others studying specific time periods. What emerges is a pattern that outlines the shifting power relations transferring control from workers to managers and the formation of a *social system in which discipline and control of people are corequisites and, at times, prerequisites of the drive for increased quantitative efficiency.*

I want to highlight briefly those aspects of radical theory that correspond to the management concerns discussed earlier.

Labor process. In *Labor and Monopoly Capital*, Harry Braverman examines the sources of the degradation of work. He explores aspects of the division of labor that attempt to remove knowledge from worker activities, and he makes an all-important distinction between this type of labor division and that found in society:

> The division of labor in society is characteristic of all known societies; the division of labor in the workshop is a special product of capitalist society. The

social division of labor divides society among occupations, each adequate to a branch of production; the detailed division of labor destroys occupations considered in this sense, and renders the worker inadequate to carry through any complete production process. In capitalism, the social division of labor is enforced chaotically and anarchically by the market, while the workshop division of labor is imposed by planning and control. . . .

While the social division of labor subdivides *society*, the detailed division of labor subdivides *humans*, and the species, the subdivision of the individual, and while the subdivision of society may enhance the individual, when carried on without regard to human capabilities and needs, is a crime against the person and against humanity.[47]

Braverman's point, and that of Marx before him, is that people must be treated as whole human beings if they are to think and act for their own satisfaction and that of society. *Work that subdivides thoughts and actions is anything but natural; it is a method of social control.*

Marx explains that the difference between human labor and the activities of animals is the human ability to think and create:

A spider conducts operations that resemble those of a weaver, and a bee puts to shame many an architect in the construction of her cells. But what distinguishes the worst architect from the best of bees is this, that the architect raises his structure in imagination before he erects it in reality. At the end of every labor-process, we get a result that already existed in the imagination of the laborer at its commencement.[48]

When the activities of the head are separated from those of the hands, the result, says Marx, "attacks the individual at the very roots of his life."[49] What is done in the name of capitalist efficiency is in fact crippling for the functioning of the individual. Marx's blazing critique of the division of labor in his lifetime is picked up by Braverman in his study of Frederick Taylor's Scientific Management. Braverman explains that Taylor's principles were attempts to accomplish the following: (1) "dissociation of the labor process from the skills of the worker"; (2) "separation of conception from execution"; and (3) "use of this monopoly over knowledge to control each step of the labor process and its mode of execution."[50] The slicing of conception (thought) from execution (action) leaves the worker potentially defenseless against the encroachment of managerial rules and control.

Worker Behavior. Richard Edwards reiterates the theme of discipline and control in his contemporary studies of large bureaucratic enterprise. He finds that "three principal modes of compliance—that is, work habits or 'behavior traits' which are 'appropriate' responses to the enterprises's power and facilitate its control"—have emerged.[51] These modes of compliance mold corporate workers to demonstrate "rules orientation," "habits of dependability and predictability," and "internalization of the enterprise's values."[52] In short, corporate workers must be shaped into behavior patterns that are open to observation and quantification. Workers who sufficiently "internalize" the corporate goals do not need to be forced or coerced into following orders. Workers who demonstrate "good work habits" such as dependability and punctuality require less supervision.

Samuel Bowles and Herbert Gintis trace the roots of these behavior patterns within the school system, describing how the school systems have been geared to produce disciplined workers—those who exhibit "appropriate" attitudes about work.[53] Indeed, calls for these work habits have been heard from corporate managers who complain that, although workers may enter the labor market with more years of schooling, they still lack the required work habits. Much of the criticism of today's schooling centers precisely around this point: schools may be failing to produce people who can read, write, and compute—but, according to management, they are also failing to produce "good" worker behavior traits.

Managerial attempts to shape appropriate work behavior are aimed at molding the consciousness of workers. When Marxists use terms like "class struggle," they mean more than the potential battle between those who control the wealth and those who work—for this struggle also involves controlling one's own consciousness. There may be nothing wrong with obedience, dependability, and predictability. All societies require some behavioral guidelines to frame the relations between people. The problem, however, is the purpose to which these behavioral patterns are put. Behavior control that focuses on inserting interchangeable individuals into interchangeable job functions clearly delimits individual power. The powerlessness and helplessness felt by many workers is intensified by rigid job ladders that keep workers on the "right" behavioral tracts. Jeremy Brecher and Tim Costello interpret promotional hierarchies within large corporations:

> While ostensibly benefiting the employees, they actually serve as a means to motivate workers to work in the present by dangling before them the carrot of future advancement. At its most effective, this technique can lead workers not only to perform as their employers desire, but to adopt the attitudes they think their employers would like them to hold.[54]

Not only do job ladders help to motivate workers, they also provide a mechanism for dividing and conquering the work force:

> It can likewise turn workers against one another in a scramble for each other's jobs. Many of the conflicts on the job between different age, race, sex and other groups grow out of competition for the more favored ranges of the job hierarchy. Job stratification even has powerful effects off the job, determining much of the inequality of income and status that mark our society at large.[55]

Shape of Management Organization. To the extent that

management strategies are able to strip workers of their knowledge and their power, this process increases worker dependence on the coordination and control functions of management.[56] Divided work performed by divided workers must be put back together in some organized way. Today, business organization is characterized by hierarchical structures that are arranged according to bureaucratic procedures. According to Max Weber, bureaucracy is a structure with clearly defined social relations as well as formal rules and procedures. The formality of the structure can be used to build efficient operations:

> To modern ears, the claim that a bureaucracy moves with greater speed and precision than any other type of organization may seem strange. We are accustomed to think of bureaucracies as slow and inefficient, bound down by red tape. However, Weber's point was that bureaucracy substituted a rule of rational law for rule by the whims of those who happened to be in charge.[57]

Richard Edwards argues that the "efficiency" of bureaucratic enterprise lies, not in its claim to speed or output, but rather in its control of the relations within the structure. He sees bureaucratic control as a means to institutionalize power:

> With bureaucratic control power became institutionalized by vesting it in official positions or roles and permitting its exercise only according to prescribed rules, procedures, and expectations; rules governing the exercise of power were elements of the work criteria defining supervisors' jobs. Since there were formally established criteria for evaluating the exercise of power, it also was made accountable to *topdown* control.[58]

These "imbedded power relationships" reinforce the objectives of management science. They create an environment where predictability and reliability are the keynotes of performance. Emphasizing *depersonalized* relations, this

form of organization gives the illusion that rules and procedures have replaced control by "the boss," but, in reality, the
institutionalization of rules and procedures serves to mask
and strengthen the power of the "boss."[59]

Technology. Another area masking power is technology.
The importance of demystifying its role cannot be under-
rated. If anything reinforces worker images of helplessness,
it is the notion that "the machine did it." Coupled with the
idea that fragmented jobs result from depersonalized administration, the ideology of technological determinism is a
pervasive form of social control. Brecher and Costello
describe it this way:

> It is an illusion, however, that machinery per se
> dictates such a pattern of work. Rather it is the way
> in which today's machines are designed and used. If
> workers controlled the design and use of the ma-
> chinery, it would be possible to create far different
> schedules and rhythms. The subservience of many
> workers to "their" machines is a product of their
> subservience to their employers. *It results from the
> deliberate effort of employers to use machines as a
> way to control those who work for them.*[60]

More than one hundred years ago Karl Marx wrestled
with the same illusion and came to the same conclusions.
Although most of his opponents and some of his supporters
have labeled him a "technological determinist," his writings
taken as a whole demonstrate that "Marx is insistent that
technology has to be understood as a social process."[61] He
saw technology as an extension of the objectives of a society.
Clearly, no imperative labels it "good" or "evil." For Marx,
history is the interaction of the social relations of production and the forces of production. The social relations
outline the power relations in the society and specify, on the
base of those power relations, the organization of work.
Forces include the tools and mechanisms of the society. In
other words, the forces, of which technology is a part, are
geared to insure a status quo in the power base of the
economy. Both technology and the social relations of

production are closely bound together. As one changes, so does the other: "Social relations are closely bound up with productive forces. In acquiring new productive forces men change their mode of production; and in changing their mode of production, in changing the way of earning their living, they change all their social relations."[62]

The relationship between the social relations and forces is a dialectical one; it describes the push and pull of historical developments. David Noble continues Marx's logic into the twentieth century: "Insofar as the emerging capitalist relations between classes make possible the creation of a social surplus, they make possible as well the development of more sophisticated productive forces which both *reflect and reinforce the social relations.*"[63] Certainly, technological developments do not arrive on the work scene by themselves. Like the organization of labor and the organization of management functions, they are shaped to discipline workers so that predictability and control become self-governing aspects of the workplace.

Management Theory and Data Processing

Computer technology affects and is affected by the functions of the company using it.[64] The organization, as analyzed by Edward Tomeski, is composed of three types of resources— human, physical, and informational. He explains that information technology plays the key role in finding the right "mix" of these resources. Information technology involves more than just computers, for it is concerned with methods and procedures for coordinating and controlling the systematic use of information. He defines information technology as "the disciplines of planning, systems design, systems analysis, operations research and computer programming.[65] In other words, it is the harnessing of information to the objectives of management science. Both the computer and the computer worker are involved in this process.

Information technology requires prior planning and analysis. Before information can be used effectively by management it must be studied and shaped to fit the needs of the organization. In a case study of United Airlines, for example, it was found that computers would not affect the organization as much as systems analysis, which must *precede* computer use.[66] C. Wright Mills found this to be the case (before the introduction of computers) in his study of white-collar work.

> Under the impetus of concentrated enterprise and finance, when the office was enlarged during the first decade of the twentieth century, a need was felt for *systematic arrangement of business facts*. . . . As the army of clerks grew, they were divided into departments, specialized in function, and thus, *before machines were introduced* on any scale, socially rationalized. The work was reorganized in a systematic and divided manner. . . .

> Thus, machines did not impel the development, but rather the development demanded machines, many of which were actually developed especially for tasks already socially created.[67]

In the first decade of computer use, the only applications that could be adapted to computer processing were those, such as payroll and accounting procedures, in which the work processes had already undergone extensive division of labor and specialization. Computerization of a process requires that the steps in that process be defined in *extreme detail* so that computer programs can be written that will imitate the actions of the workers. *As long as the work process is controlled by the private knowledge of the workers involved, the application of information technology is impossible.*

Information technology, therefore, reinforces the "increased emphasis on quantification of information . . . and attention to making explicit the assumptions" used in decision models. The upshot is an organization that can be controlled and predicted because decision-making becomes increasingly "*rationalized and explicit and less and less in-*

tuitive."[68] Running throughout management literature are arguments for prior analysis and rationalization of functions in order to remove arbitrary judgments and increase predictability.

The impersonal nature of bureaucratic rules for predictability and control affects workers and the work process. For the individual workers, information technology means an increase in the depersonalized aspects of the job as well as greater management control over their actions through "time discipline," which influences the pace of production and the physical mobility of the worker.[69] The labor process is affected by the demands of prior rationalization, which result in further specialization, standardization, simplification, and speed-up.

Information technology has also influenced organizational structure by renewing interest in the issue of decentralization versus centralization.[70] Prior to the introduction of information technology most large firms relied on centralized structures in order to exert overt control over all operations. Decentralized operational functions became more attractive when upper management could "monitor continuously . . . the effectiveness of the decentralized units in contributing to the overall corporate objectives."[71] The continuous monitoring became possible as operational functions and decision-making patterns became more precisely defined. Systems analysis played the critical role in defining functions, and computers provided the "monitor" by allowing continuous (or at least routine) reports to be generated for management.

In addition to centralized and decentralized organizations, a matrix or multidimensional structure has emerged, which lets the firm control all *policy* decisions centrally at the top level and "pass down" the *operational* and pre-established decisions to middle and lower management.[72] This synthesis gives upper management the power to control and predict all essential policy from a central vantage point and at the same time delegate the routine operational decisions to decentralized units. Such structures are supported by distributed data processing whereby each corporate department and/or function can have its own small-scale computing power for processing its routine functions, effectively distributing computer use throughout the firm.

The application of information technology hinges on the procedures for systematizing the decision-making process. The manner in which information is collected and organized is not dictated by specific requirements of computers but by the needs of the organization: "The structure of business organizations and the content of management jobs within them reflect the organization's process of decision-making and the flows of information used to reach those decisions."[73] Herbert Simon's studies of decision-making lead him to believe that information technology can be increasingly applied to decision-making theory. As decisions are made more routine, they can be incorporated into computerized processing:

> An organization can be pictured as a three-layer cake. In the bottom layer, we have the basic work processes. . . . In the middle layer, we have the programmed decision-making processes, the processes that govern the day-to-day operation of the manufacturing and distribution system. In the top layer, we have the nonprogrammed decision making processes, the processes that are required to design and redesign the entire system, to provide it with its basic goals and objectives, and to monitor its performance.
>
> Automation of data processing and decision-making will not change this fundamental three-part structure. It may, by bringing about a more explicit formal description of the entire system, make the relations among the parts clear and more explicit.[74]

Management science builds on the foundations of Scientific Management and human relations theories, but extends their limits by including new methods for controlling complex organizations. Chief among these new methods is the concept that management must go beyond cost-reduction of individual functions and beyond morale of individual workers to the development of models for predicting and controlling all barriers to continued growth.

By providing the quantitative tools and analytical methods, management science has become a developing set of theories that allows managers to make trade-offs between objectives—objectives that seek to decrease cost and at the same time minimize labors' resistance. For data-processing managers the literature of management science provides the framework for remodeling occupational change.

The application of management theory to the problems of managing data-processing workers did not fully begin until the 1960s when the increasing number of workers and the functions they provided began having an impact on the firm. From that time to the present, the issues concerning management of data-processing workers have paralleled the central issues in management theory. Of course, management practitioners differ in their approaches to the "how-to-manage" question, but they are in agreement in their acceptance of the philosophy and techniques of management science. Generally, the literature of data-processing management perceives that the knowledge and skills of data-processing workers must be rationalized so that it can be more fully controlled by management.[75] The main debate in this literature centers on the question of whether computer work is similar to other occupations and, therefore, whether computer workers can be controlled by the same policies. Some authors stress the fact that the intangible nature of the product—computerized system—hinders the ability to control data-processing workers. Others feel that data-processing workers can be entirely eliminated, and with them the unorthodox problems they create.[76] The main line of literature, however, follows the path of management theory, borrowing and adapting methodology to the "growing pains" of computer work processes.

If the problems of managing labor are complex, then those involved in data-processing management are indeed extraordinary. During the 1960s most computer projects could be characterized as overbudget, late, and ineffective.[77] Complaints centered on the actions of computer workers rather than on the functioning of computer equipment. *In a sense, the machine was ready, but the work process was not.* Managers worried that their investment in computers could not pay off until "computers and their applications can be managed reliably in an economic sense."[78] But this economic accountability was difficult as long as computer workers controlled computer skills and the computer equipment. A report by the McKinsey consulting firm warned that companies could not "abdicate control of their computers to staff specialists."[79] Computer workers seemed to have sprung up as the keepers of the technology gate. Over and over again management literature warned that as long as the techniques of data processing remained locked in workers' heads, the workers would continue to make "independent decisions" and thus avoid fiscal control by management.[80]

By borrowing the tools and theories of management science, data-processing management was better equipped to address this issue. Step by step, the process of observing, defining, and quantifying data-processing tasks was begun. In general, it was agreed that these procedures were necessary *before* management could begin to tackle the question of cost reduction. Data processing was not the first "intangible" occupation to go through this transformation. David Noble outlines the same developments in the transformation of the engineering profession at the turn of the century.[81] Indeed, in order to reach the objective of cost reduction, it was clear that the prerequisite was control, which according to management science had to include the ability to measure the steps in the labor process and the actions of the workers.

Management science recognizes that the accomplishment of its objectives is not easy, for trade-offs have to be made between achieving straightforward quantifiable efficiency (more output) and keeping the reactions and demands of workers under control. In scientific terms, for every action there is a reaction. The literature of management science attempts to give managers the tools to overlay this environment with the identification and control of variables that allow them to predict and thus plan for continued growth. As Reinhard Bendix argues, "all ideologies of management have in common the effort to interpret the exercise of authority in a favorable light."[82]

But the scientific sound of "controlling variables" and "predicting reactions" masks the very real changes that occur when management seeks to implement policies of control. Management theory indicates that division of labor and hierarchical structures are inevitable, but when we examine these processes on the shopfloor we find that they are superimposed on a totally different form of social organization.

Part II looks at the four types of change that have been used by management to alter data-processing work. The changes reflect attempts by management to rationalize the labor process, to control the behavior of workers, to mold data processing into the bureaucratic organizational pattern, and to shape the technology to meet management objectives. In general, there is no fixed historical progression to the four forms of management control. In some situations ideological control of worker behavior has had to precede work process changes, and in other situations just the reverse has been true. Sometimes, management organizational structure has had to be remolded before work process changes could be implemented. Often these strategies appear inseparable, for they are brought into practice at the same time. The choice of strategy and point of time at which it is used are, of course, influenced by the business environment of the firm.

In the data-processing field, division of labor seems to have been the historical prelude to other forms of change. Division of labor and work process rationalization were not successful in increasing worker productivity until they were accompanied by other changes, most noticeably those aimed at controlling worker behavior.

Each strategy will be viewed from an historical perspective within the data-processing field, looking at management theory, worker response, and the synthesis of management practice. Although management practice is usually modified by the reactions of workers, management objectives hold fast to those outlined by management theory. As the theories of management are applied by the practitioners of middle to lower management the social relations of the workplace are built. These social relations emerge in an environment in which increased quantitative efficiency (output) is matched and molded to fit qualitative efficiency (social control). The way work and workers are organized reflects the power relations within a society.

PART

II

Shopfloor
Practice

CHAPTER

4

Labor Process

Representing the "hard-line" or efficiency argument in programming management, Dick Brandon, in the 1960s, set the stage for controlling the work process:

> The normal employer-employee relationship, which in part depends on the fear of termination or disciplinary action, does not exist. . . .

> It is not at all uncommon for a programmer to threaten resignation, while simultaneously generating the type of undocumented programs that increase management's dependence on him.

> Thus he is in a position of strength from which he can (and in the aggregate, often does) use mild blackmail to achieve greater status, money or dominance over management.[1]

In data processing the way that work is done has changed over the last twenty years. Work has been divided and fragmented, separating "conception" tasks such as programming from "execution" chores such as operations. Formal standards have been introduced in an effort to specify how work should be done and how much should be expected from each worker. The tools of the trade have also been simplified in order to make both programming and operations into less skilled and therefore less expensive jobs. Operating systems and programming languages, for example, are tools that were developed to increase productivity.

This process, which Kraft aptly calls "deskilling," has occurred over the push and pull of worker reaction to labor process change.[2] Sometimes programmers and operators welcome a new standard or simplification procedure because it gave them a new "skill," albeit a temporary one. At other times they resisted management attempts to standardize their actions because it was clear that their knowledge and control were being taken away. Whether these changes were introduced by "hard-line" or "soft-line" managers, they have resulted in more cut and dried work processes.

Each time a new tool or standard was introduced workers were told that routine tasks were being removed from their jobs in order to free their minds for more creative endeavors. The argument is an old and often abused one. For workers caught in the changing work process, the changes clearly did not upgrade their specific jobs. In addition, these changes were theoretically supposed to make the workers more productive, yet in most data-processing tasks increased efficiency does not seem to have occurred. Indeed, the issue of whether data-processing labor has become more efficient is seriously challenged by management today.[3] Management's attempts to change the work process contrast with workers' perceptions of what has happened to them and their jobs.[4]

Division of Labor

In early computer installations almost all work from problem analysis through computer operation was done by the programmer. One programmer put it this way:

> I remember that in the fifties and early sixties I was a "jack of all trades." As a programmer I got to deal with the whole process. I would think through a

problem, talk to the clients, write my own code, and
operate the machine. I loved it—particularly the
chance to see something through from beginning to
end.

Most programmers tended to see themselves as free-
wheeling, independent craftspeople: "In those days [late
fifties and early sixties] we really had control. Management
never understood what we were doing and we really didn't
care. It was fun and what we were doing made us feel
important—we felt like we were accomplishing something."

But the "jack of all trades" did not fit within the already
rationalized corporate structure. In a case study of programmers in England, sociologist Andrew Pettigrew found
that the introduction of these multi-skilled programmers
caused a "culture shock" for other employees and for
management. Pettigrew described the situation this way:

> In fact, their strange work time-table and casual
> dress attracted criticism. The programmers also
> disrupted company rules about clocking on and off.
> This together with the rewards their market position
> afforded them at such a comparatively young age,
> created problems within the company status
> system.[5]

Middle and lower level managers who attempted to
interact with the programming work force reacted with the
same criticism.[6] Management embarked on a program to
separate the decision-making tasks of programming from
the more routine physical tasks of operating the computer.
This kind of division of labor had proved quite successful in factory production, as one which in Marx's description, required a division "between the hand labor and
head labor."[7]

Dividing conceptual tasks like programming from
executable work such as operations did not occur throughout the industry at the same time. Its first enforced
appearance seems to have been in the aerospace industry in
the mid-1950s. Many large companies, under contract to
the military, borrowed military procedures and applied

them to computer applications. One worker describes his programming shop for an aircraft company in 1956:

> It was a "closed shop," programmers were never allowed in the machine room. We [the programmers] really hated that part because it took us forever to get anything corrected. We would code a program and send it to the keypunch section, after three or four days we would get it back, make our corrections, and send it back to keypunch. When it looked "clean" [correct], it would be sent to the operators. We might have to wait two days to get it back, make our corrections, and start the process all over again.

> My friends who worked for commercial companies didn't have the aggravation of the closed shop. They were allowed to run their own programs, and they got a lot more done.

Early division of labor also had a strong foothold at AT&T. The company's existing job classification schemes were placed intact within the new computer department. AT&T avoided the "culture shock" problem by labeling all computer positions "clerical" and continuing standard recruitment practice of hiring women for clerical slots. Even before the installation of the third-generation computer system (IBM's 360), programmers were kept out of the machine room. AT&T's extensively divided labor and fully rationalized procedures were unusual for their time.

Separation of the "head" labor of programming from the "hand" labor of operations took several computer "generations" to become enforceable. Programmers were reluctant to give up the fun and skill involved in correcting their programs at the machine. This process, which is called "hands-on debugging," was for many programmers the high point of their day:

> The "hands-on" time was really the best part of programming. We would get one, maybe two "shots" [times on the computer] per day, and it was

during this time that you would actually get to see whether the logic of the program worked. It was like trying to beat the machine at its own game. It was a challenge.

For operators, enforced division of labor represented a step down:

Without a knowledge of programming a computer operator is just like any other machine operator. I went into operations because it was exciting and had the status of being an "IBM" job—that really impressed people. But when we were told that we couldn't even help programmers with their programs, well—the job began to lose its excitement and status.

The message to operators was the old Frederick Taylor adage, "You're not being paid to think, just do your job."

In many smaller installations, where the doors to the machine room were not locked, the boundary between conception and execution was unenforceable. In most cases workers consider overlapping functions to be not only more enjoyable but also more productive. One programmer summarized the frustrations of many others in her description of the problem: "As a programmer I could get a lot more done without all the rules that prevent me from using the machine room. The operators—they also complain that they waste a great deal of time because they don't really know what's going on with the programs."

Separating operations still left programmers with a wide range of skills that, in essence, kept them in the driver's seat. Pettigrew's study found that although programmers had to interact with people throughout the company, their "values, work patterns and dress" were starkly different:

Faced with increasing hostility between programmers and user departments, the company decided to set up an Organization and Methods Department [forerunner to Systems Analysis Dept.]. This department's role was to act as a link between

programmers and user departments and generally
to translate the company's needs into computer
terms.[8]

In the eyes of the rest of the company programmers were
seen as technicians and distrusted for their "unusual"
behavior. For managers, programmer behavior created a
company-wide problem. Managers from other departments
who attempted to request services from the programming
staff were usually confronted with jargon they did not
understand. Their distrust and lack of control over the
programming work force led to the development of
programs that did not fit management needs. From a
management standpoint business communication had to be
divided from technical orientation. Systems analysts would
be hired to communicate with management and deal with
business problems; programmers could then be left to their
technical details. The process follows Herbert Simon's
breakdown of three categories of decision-making.[9]
Systems analysts interact with users, define problems, and
engage in the more creative aspects of "head" labor.
Programmers carry out the coding functions, which, like
Simon's middle layer, translate "programmed decision-
making" into machine instructions. Operators perform the
most routine and repetitive actions, which, when fully
rationalized, become "hand" or manual labor.

Marshall Meyer, another social scientist studying data-
processing departments, found a similar reason for the split.
Meyer looked at 254 government data-processing departments and concluded that analyst titles were inserted into
the organization to help bridge the gap between technical
and management functions. The problem Meyer found was
that high level managers were caught in positions in which
they had to request services of lower level technicians. Not
only did this represent a breach in hierarchical structure, but
managers came away empty-handed. Programmers could
and often did refuse management requests, on the basis of
technical "expertise."[10] It's not as though programmers
willfully misbehaved like children in the face of authority.

Retaining technical details in their heads and withholding them from the rest of the company are examples of common actions on the part of groups who feel threatened. Like other craft workers they did the things that seemed necessary for the survival of their skill.

As we have seen, management policy and its implementation take time to evolve. Creating the ranks of systems analysts did not result in programmers relinquishing analytical tasks. Pettigrew's study found that it took close to a decade before each group had its own identity. At first programmers continued to dominate both activities, for it was they who had the technical skill, and in the early computer days "much did depend on the expertise of the programmers."[11] The introduction of computer operating system software helped to make computers easier to use and thus shake loose the programmers' claim to exclusive expertise. In addition, as systems analysts were increasingly recruited for their knowledge of business functions, they began to evolve their own craft, one that could not be dominated by technical programmer skill.

Management initiated the split between the "conception" functions of systems analysis and the "execution" functions of programming in order to control worker activity and thereby partially control the service provided by this group. Systems analysts, who as a group represented the higher level function and dressed and acted in compliance with company policy, were given the higher salaries. Programmers were paid less and placed "at the end of the workflow." A programmer in Pettigrew's study had this to say: "It's a farce; they [the analysts] sort out the general systems and leave us to sort out all the mess-ups. People see the mistakes at the programming stage though it may be Systems fault."[12]

By creating the distinction between these two jobs, management had in fact created two separate groups whose insecurities in the corporate environment led them to vie for power. Programmers complained that analysts did not know anything about computers, and analysts grumbled that programmers knew nothing about the business world.

Both complaints were grounded in some degree of truth, but the actual separation of functions strengthened these distinctions.

I found that by the 1970s the roots of their jobs were not visible to most newcomers in the field. A programmer in a large bank comments on her position today: "I'm a programmer, I don't really know anything about systems analysis. The Systems analysts all seem to run around and talk about business problems I don't understand. I like my work though, I wouldn't want to change places." A Systems analyst describes his job: "I like to talk with users and think that I'm really very good at it. Some of the guys around here are good at technical details, and they go in for programming. Me, my expertise is in understanding user's business problems."

Pettigrew concluded that "the division of labor cannot be legislated; it must be worked out at each locale."[13] What his study ignores, though, is that workers did not *initiate* the division. Their struggle for power and definition has been in *reaction* to management policy to divide labor in order to control actions and cut costs. Having created separate and unequal status among data-processing workers, management has difficulty putting the pieces back together. An employment agent that I interviewed indicated that this is a growing problem today: "At a time like this when the industry is again growing very fast and there aren't enough bodies to do the work, the companies want data-processing workers who can do a little bit of everything; analysis, programming, even some operating. They are hard to find!"

It's no wonder workers are hard to find, for the effects of the divide and conquer policies have spread. Over the last decade each category of labor-power has been recruited and trained in a different manner from the others. As would be expected, antagonisms have developed and have been allowed to fester between these groups. Systems analysts blamed programmers, programmers blamed operators, and operators, whenever possible, accused keypunch operators. Individually, they were and often are the best of friends, but as groups they are bound by company-wide policies of competition. Competition is an integral part of capitalist management strategy. It not only keeps workers motivated toward achieving more, it also helps focus attention away from management.

Standardization of Tasks

Because the "hand" labor of operations was more clearly defined it was easier for management to set standards and measure performance. As the hardware and software were designed to include more and more operator functions, the pace of operations was increasingly monitored by the machines. But this was not so in the early 1960s. An operations shopfloor supervisor talked about his work for a large bank at this time:

> When I took over the shop there were twelve guys working a full shift plus overtime to turn out the reports for trust accounts, stock transfer, and the central loan accounting for the branches. The problem was that these guys were pretty arrogant and thought that they were essential. It was night shift and they would mess around all the time and then demand overtime because the work wasn't finished. Of course the bank officers didn't know what to do with them because they didn't know anything about data processing. Well, I turned the shop around—I codified and defined all the jobs and within four months that shift could operate with five guys and no overtime.

He described how, as a new supervisor, he made the shop more efficient:

> I knew that as long as the guys kept information about what they did from management that they could get away with being "essential." I started by observing the shopfloor and writing up descriptions of what each guy did. Of course I had to get their confidence to do this. I offered them "time off" as a reward and they loved it. If they got their job done in

six hours instead of the full eight of the shift I let
them go home early but still get paid for the shift.
For those guys who really needed overtime, I saw to
it that there was some to spread around.

His experience, although maybe not his "success," was fairly
common during this period. Bank data-processing installations were batch-processing centers where large volumes
of data were collected during the day and run at night.
Batch-processing differs from continuous flow in that the
groups of data require "set-up and take-down time," which
means that the control of the machine is actually determined
by the operator setting up the jobs. Standards for job set-up
were all the more critical because the "operators had total
control of machine utilization. If an operator left a machine
idle he was not only wasting his time but costing the
company a lot in lost computer time."

Shopfloor supervisors are rarely trained in either
management theory or management tactics, yet in so many
circumstances they effectively copy the strategies of their
managerial superiors. As one operations supervisor explained, given his chance to act in a responsible position, he
"just wanted to see if the work could be done the right way":

I never studied management and I think of myself as
a humanist. I really cared about the people working
for me. Except for the "dead wood"—you know,
the guys who never really would do anything—I
made sure that everyone was taken care of. When I
proved that we could do the job with less people the
good guys were all transferred to other jobs—in
fact, most were promoted.

My policy was this: once I established the rules for
each job step I told the guys that if they did it my way
they could get the rewards of going home early and
maybe even promotion. I rotated the job steps so
that everyone knew each other's tasks and no one
could claim that they were special. They liked the
variety. There was only one fellow who was a real

> problem, he refused to let anyone else learn his job. I paired him with the biggest, toughest guy in the department, who threatened to throw a metal tray of cards at him—well, he shaped up.

Definitions of operations tasks were a prerequisite for development of more sophisticated software. As the tasks were defined and standardized, they were programmed, thus bypassing the decisions that had been made by operators.

Programming standards were also called for.[14] A programming project manner in the 1960s describes what this meant in terms of his job:

> No one knew what was going on—certainly not the managers. But even the programmers and systems analysts were confused. There were no standards for doing anything—coding, testing, documenting— they were all done the way each person felt like it, or in fact, they were not done at all. Some programmers would write amazing but unintelligible code. You couldn't run a project that way.

His motives, like those of his counterparts in operations, were oriented toward what he saw as "enlightened" management:

> The way I saw it was that I really wanted to put together the best project that I could. You know, something that I could feel proud of. Well, I couldn't do that if everybody went off and did their own thing. I had to coordinate the putting together of the programs into a useful system. In order to do that I had to divide the job up into standard modules so that I could tell when each task would get done, and what it would do.

Although he developed written standards for each task within the project, he found that they were by and large ignored. Developing standards and implementing them were two different things:

> Programmers never documented [wrote down]

what it was that their program was to do. It was the
same with setting up testing procedures and test
data. When the whole system was put together, we
never knew if it really worked because nothing got
written down. The programmers always claimed to
be too busy.

Probably the largest body of literature for programming
management deals with strategies for standardizing procedures so that *managers can estimate* the time a job takes.
Everything from measurement formulae such as kilo-
babbages and production rates to manpower-utilization
indexes to lines-of-code-per-day has been devised to make
project estimation a management science rather than a
programmer art.[15] The most important factor to control is
the project "due date"—will the project be completed in the
promised time? Programming first-line and middle
managers, that is those directly responsible, always feel as
though they are caught "with their pants down" when
programmers commit them to a due date that is not met.
According to management theory, it is the manager who is
responsible for delivering the service. How then can the
manager "deliver" what is within the control of the
programmer?

Back in the sixties we just never made our due dates.
I don't think that as a programmer I ever made one.
It wasn't held against us since it was common
practice and back then where were they going to get
someone else to do the work?

Now, as a manager, I see it differently. Of course,
now most of the standards have long been established so that I know how many lines of code to
expect from the average programmer, and they
either do it or they are out.

First-line and middle managers are still complaining
about the lack of formal standards in programming.
Programmers see the problem growing out of a variety of
causes. One programmer, for example, revealed a common
fear:

> We never really established this as a policy, but what kind of job security would we have if we wrote everything down the way they wanted us to? We didn't like it when things got too out of control, but on the other hand would you see to it that your job was so standardized that it could be done by a monkey?

Another programmer described the experience:

> After you've been doing it for a while, coding gets boring. Especially after they divide up the project into so many modules that you don't know what you're doing relative to the whole system. So partly it's to preserve our sanity—we do things our own way and don't document it. Anyway, documenting is the most boring part of all.

Some managers see programmer noncompliance as sabotage against which they must carefully plan. But managers who grow out of the programming ranks usually know that such actions are aspects of resistance to be expected when standardization is emphasized, as one explains:

> When I was a programmer, I did the same thing. It wasn't as if we all sat down and planned exactly how many lines of code we would do per day—it was more like the fact that we *informally established group standards* for ourselves. I guess peer pressure saw to it that our standards and not theirs were enforced.

> Anyway, when you are a programmer you don't know what's on the planning horizon. If you finish one program too fast they will just give you another one to do.

At a recent conference on programmer productivity[16] a group of data-processing managers informally expressed their opinions about the programming process today. One remarked:

> The industry now has generally accepted guidelines

for what kind of productivity to expect at each step
in the project life cycle. It's all units of "executable
lines of code" which can be delivered per day.
It's funny, but on the average the number of lines of
executable [workable] code has remained at about
ten for the last decade.

When asked if this was strange considering the fact that it
was such a low number, another jumped to respond:

Of course it's ridiculously low productivity, but at
least we know what to expect and we don't get
caught promising upper management things we
can't deliver.

My programmers code at four times the national
average, which makes me look really good.

A third summarized the situation:

Look if we're really honest about it, we know that
programmers don't work as hard as they could.
Right now they've cornered us into these comparatively low productivity estimates, but we all get
something out of it. I can promise my managers
something, it's definable—and they [the program-
mers] know where they stand.

Simplification of Tools

Division of labor and standardization of procedures
establish what management literature calls the "min-max"
limits for controlling the work process. They lay down
expectations for "how much" and "what" will be done, but
they do not necessarily specify "how" it will be accomplished. If data processing was to be transformed from
an art into a science, as management journals urged, then
sharper tools were necessary to simplify work procedures.
    Many developments in the field have helped managers
simplify work tasks and thus better control the work
process. Probably the most significant in terms of long-

range effect on the degradation of skill has been the use of operating systems, programming languages, and structured coding. The key to the success of these devices has been removal of decision-making from the workers' control, incorporating it directly into the computer system software.

Operating systems are a form of super-software that monitors and controls the flow of processing to and from the machine. Until the mid-sixties scheduling of machine use was the bailiwick of the operator:

> As an operator I was a form of god. I really had power over the machine, and even over the programmers using it. For example, if there was a large payroll coming in and I knew that it would take several hours to print it, I would leave the machine idle so that it wouldn't get tied up waiting for the big job. Sometimes I would give blocks of time to the programmers to play with, and other times, if we weren't busy, the other operators and I would play with it ourselves.

Operating systems, which are made up of programs, simplify the procedures operators have to follow and provide both programmers and operators with more complete monitoring messages. Their central function is to increase the efficiency, or throughput, of data processing by allocating the machine's resources. An operator comments on the impact this function has had on operators: "I think that the source of OS [IBM's first large-scale operating system] was IBM's way of saying that it's time to take random scheduling out of operator hands and put it in the machine." Operating systems were introduced to workers as an advancement that would remove the more routine functions, leaving both operators and programmers more time for increased skills and creativity.

The contradiction between "taking scheduling out of operator hands" and increasing the operators' marketable skills was not clear at first. Each new operating system brought new skills and challenges to the programmers and operators using it. For operators, it may have taken away their ultimate "godlike" power over the machine, but it gave them something in return: "We used to call OS the mighty Wizard of Oz. It could do so many wonderful things and it was a challenge to use it."

As with other changes in the field, it took a "computer generation" before the "mighty Wizard" was smoothly performing an increasing number of operator functions. As the functions of operating systems expanded, so did the control languages used to coordinate their functions. Since operating systems are programs, their development and maintenance have been taken away from operators and given to a new subspecialty group called systems programmers. Today, operators manipulate the manual aspects of the machine, but they are rarely schooled in the control language that performs the functions their predecessors used to do. They cannot even speak the language of the machines they operate.

Many managers agree that simplifying the work process has gone too far. The operating system that took control away from the operator also took away all traces of decision-making practice. Forgetting the management decisions that allowed this to happen, many managers tend to blame the victim: "Give me an operator who knows what he's doing. The situation in my shop is really ridiculous—if anything goes wrong, which you know always happens, the operators are too dumb to fix it. They don't even know how to fix a JCL [Job Control Language] error." By 1967, in an article entitled "Ten Years of Progress?" *Datamation* magazine concluded that "the development of operating systems reduced the necessary level of training for those who used them." Measures such as "idle time," "set-up time," and "re-run time," became vestiges of the past *as operating systems made processing more continuous and less dependent on human intervention.*[17]

Programmers were also confronted by the contradictions in the design of operating systems. On the one hand, they needed increased skill to take full advantage of the sophistications offered by the system; on the other hand, they lost skill as routines like input/output processing, which they had formerly coded, were included in the software: "The operating system was supposed to give us more time to write 'creative' code. It did take away the more repetitive coding functions, but it sure didn't give us more time for creativity. Managers just had more things for us to do!"

Programming, or problem-oriented, languages simplify the coding process for the programmer. They are designed to "allow programmers with less training to do more useful work."[18] They accomplish this by isolating the repetitive and routine aspects of program logic and condensing them into a set of easier-to-use instructions. Philip Kraft outlines this in his book on programmers: "Similar attempts to routinize work have been made by managers of the most diverse workplaces. The common denominator has been the desire to substitute less skilled and therefore less expensive workers for more skilled and more expensive workers."[19] In effect, programming languages are to programmers what operating systems are to operators: they simplify the workers' interaction with the machine.

The search for easier-to-use programming languages began in the mid-1950s when managers found that they could not train the increasing number of programmers needed by industry. For managers the problem required "trading machine time and efficiency for software that is easier to use with the programmers on hand."[20] The management objective was to increase programmer productivity and, whenever possible, bypass the programmer completely.

The first successful programming language was FORTRAN, which was oriented toward scientific problem-solving. It let scientists with relatively little training in programming write instructions to solve their own problems. It was followed by a language called COBOL, which enabled programmers to code business problems in a series of English-like instructions. Although neither language was successful in replacing the programmer, they both did cut significantly into training time.

Canned, or prewritten, application languages, have

further simplified the coding process. The more routine applications—accounts receivables, payrolls, general ledgers, and standard business functions in general—have programs already written to handle their processing. Some are so standardized that they are ready to run; the operator or data-entry clerk merely enters the data and the results are processed. Others require a sort of extended application language, for which the programmer or coder enters certain codes to adapt the package to the requirements of the shop. Philip Kraft comments on their advantages for managers: "It means being able to buy or rent a ready-made program which is, he [the user] hopes, a tested and proved product, without the bother and expense of employing highly-skilled software experts to design, write, test, modify, maintain and update an *ad hoc* solution to a unique problem."[21]

Since programming languages theoretically offered programmers the chance to replace repetitive tasks with more challenging work, they were warmly received. In addition, as new languages were introduced, most large companies retrained their programmers, thus increasing their marketable skills. Learning new languages was a challenge and a change of pace:

> When they first trained us in COBOL I hated it. I thought that I couldn't do as many things in it as I had done in AUTOCODER (for the 1401). In AUTOCODER I really could get to know the machine, but I couldn't do that in COBOL.
>
> At any rate, I got used to COBOL and it turned out to be a challenge to learn to use it well. I was sent to IBM school and that too was fun. It turned out that I was really glad that they trained me in COBOL because it was in demand. I would have been dead [in terms of finding another job] if all I knew was AUTOCODER.

Like the contradictions posed by operating systems, the problems with programming languages were not readily apparent at first. As long as learning new languages was treated as skill-upgrading in the labor market, the effects as a deskilling agent were offset. *Essentially, the effect for the individual programmer has been positive—new languages bring new financial rewards—but the effect for programmers as a whole has been quite the opposite.* The more simplified the programming or application language, the more easily management has been able to replace costly programmers with lower-priced coders.

Structured programming is not so much a language as a method of using a language. The programmer is told what instructions to use, what logic to follow, and what routines to insert in the program. Management discussed the concept in the 1950s, approached it piecemeal in the 1960s, and actually implemented it in the 1970s. Its purpose is to limit the ability of programmers to make independent decisions about the organization of their programs. Kraft has this to say about structured programming:

> It freed managers from dependence on individual high-level software workers. It also made possible for the first time a genuine job-based fragmentation of labor in programming. Until structured programming, the common industry-wide division between analyst, programmer, and coder could be no more than arbitrary division of authority and control.[22]

For managers it completes the process of control that was begun by division of labor and establishment of standards. A program written along the lines of structured code has a clearly defined organization. Supervisors and first-line managers can actually read the programs and determine if programmers have undertaken what they set out to do. It removes the guesswork and gives managers another tool with which to measure and judge the performance of their employees.

Although structured programming does seem to remove decision-making and therefore skill and control from programmers, it does not seem to be greatly resisted. In my interviews with programmers I found that, like the other tools of work simplification, it is presented in such a way as to offer something in exchange for the skill it takes away. Certainly, programmers complain about the restrictions of the structure but they also enjoy being sent to training class to learn a new technique—particularly one demanded in the labor market:

> At first I thought that it was tyrannical, but I have gotten to really like it. You see, as a programmer you often have to mop up after other programmers' mistakes; debugging others' programs and modifying the programs of people who have left. Programs written in structured code are much easier to modify. It's also easier to help each other with our programs because you can follow the logic in someone else's program.

Dividing work and establishing formal standards should, according to management theory, create a less expensive work process that is easier for management to control. To a certain extent they have been successful in data-processing work, bringing about a high degree of specialization in what had been a craftlike occupation. This is most obvious at the lower levels within the data-processing hierarchy, where computer operators no longer have much control over "their" machine and junior programmers (coders) enter simplified instructions in quite routine and repetitive situations. Yet managers are not at all satisfied with the results thus far. In commenting on future trends one observer noted:

> Virtually every study in existence indicates that by 1985, 90 percent or more of the cost of data-processing will be people costs, not hardware, making data-processing the most labor-intensive industry, excepting possibly agriculture.[23]

In addition to the issue of cost, other managerial problems remain unresolved. Specialization, for example, lowers the turnover rate of workers, but also makes it more difficult to replace workers. The specialties have become so minute that workers rarely obtain experience beyond one narrow field or set of tasks. Take, for example, the issue of the computer operator. Today the operating system performs most of the functions that the operator used to do. The operating system provides faster throughput in routine functions, but in those instances where a problem arises the operator is no longer able to help. This problem comes about because the continuing division of labor also raises contradictions for the worker. Data-processing workers reacted against most of the work process changes that attempted to divide their jobs and remove skill and knowledge from their control. After more than a decade of management promise that the changes would upgrade the labor force, it is increasingly clear that rather than more "creative" work there is now just *more work* for each person to do.

Two hundred years ago Adam Smith sounded a warning about the alienating nature of division of labor: "The man whose life is spent in performing a few simple operations . . . has no occasion to exert his understanding or to exercise his invention in finding out expedients for removing difficulties . . . and generally becomes as stupid and ignorant as it is possible for a human creature to become."[24] Fragmented and repetitive jobs in the white-collar world may become no less alienating than those found in factories.

CHAPTER

5

Worker Behavior

To many observers, the on-the-job behavior of data-processing workers has changed over the last decade or so. Herbert Grosch, former president of the American Association of Computing Machinery, put it succinctly when he said, "where are all the Renaissance people—they seem to be gone from the field?"[1] An employment agent commented on the transformation:

> Back in the sixties the people in the field came from rebel stock: they were bright, creative, and loved to do things in their own way—they were pioneers. Today the people themselves seem to have become molded—molded by the organization, their education, and of course, the economic realities of losing their jobs. They are a new breed; technically knowledgeable but more plodding.[2]

While some argue that this is the result of a process of "natural selection" experienced in all occupations as they change from craft to structured discipline, it is difficult to make this form of "social Darwinism" fit, in the face of conflicting management action. Over the last fifteen years the industry's journals, newspapers, and conferences have been filled with a barrage of management "how to" tactics, which outlined in dreary detail the steps to selecting, educating, and motivating the "right" kind of data-processing employee. Even if we were to assume that most of this literature was discarded, it is difficult to believe that it had no effect on the field.

Changing the way that work is done is only part of the process. It is also necessary to change the consciousness and behavior of the worker so that there is a better "fit" of the work process, the worker, and the organization. Data-processing workers, like their counterparts in other white-collar occupations, were molded to fit corporate norms better. The intent was to create workers whose behavioral characteristics would be as predictable as the work tasks to which they would be assigned.

Managers argued that these changes were necessary in data processing because workers to fill the expanding number of jobs were in short supply. Yet the trend toward corporate norms continued, and in fact increased in tempo, during the economic crisis of the early 1970s when companies were laying off data-processing workers. Although increased efficiency was their demand, what managers were also looking for was greater control over workers themselves. Management practices sought to select, educate, and motivate the desired kind of worker. The strategies used have effected the consciousness and behavior of data-processing workers.

Selection

Most programmers of the 1950s and 1960s literally stumbled into the field; many were able to create jobs that suited their interests. A 1963 study found that 45 per cent had a math or engineering background (a suprisingly low percentage for a field that had the image of being engineering-based), and 18 per cent reported that they fell into the field by "accident."[3] A programmer relates how in the late 1950s he got into data processing:

I graduated [from] college with a math degree and

didn't really know what I wanted to do. There was this big aerospace push on, and companies were looking to hire.

They didn't know what they wanted any more than I did. It was almost as if the recruitment procedure consisted of holding a mirror under your nose; if it fogged up you were hired! Every available "body" who showed interest was sucked in.

In actual fact the recruitment procedures were more selective than they appeared to him, for very few women were recruited in the early days. The image of the field as being involved with math or science provided a preselection criterion, but general prejudice seemed to be the biggest preventive measure. A woman with a physics degree commented about the same time period: "The aerospace industry was growing fast and I really wanted to be a programmer, but women weren't 'good enough' to be programmers. We were hired at 20 per cent less than men and only allowed to set up the test cases." By the mid-1960s the self-selection criteria were beginning to dissolve in favor of planned hiring practices. As companies found that they needed large numbers of programmers, and as the tasks of programming became more standard and defined, women were recruited into the ranks.

Not women but company "misfits" were a problem in programming departments. Joseph Weizenbaum paints a rather unflattering picture of the problem, or "compulsive," programmer:

Wherever computer centers have become established, that is to say, in countless places in the United States, as well as in virtually all other industrial regions of the world, bright men [*sic*] of disheveled appearance, often with sunken glowing eyes, can be seen sitting at computer consoles, their arms tensed and waiting to fire their fingers, already poised to strike, at the buttons and keys on which their attention seems to be as riveted as a gambler's

on the rolling dice. When not so transfixed, they
often sit at tables strewn with computer printouts
over which they pore like possessed students of a
cabalistic text. . . . Their rumpled clothes, their
unwashed and unshaven faces, and their uncombed
hair all testify that they are oblivious to their bodies
and to the world in which they move. They exist, at
least when so engaged, only through and for the
computers. These are computer bums, compulsive
programmers. They are an international phenomenon.[4]

Weizenbaum, generally considered a humanist, describes in
no less detail the situation about which hard-line managers
like Brandon complain when they argue that programmers
are "excessively independent, egocentric, and slightly
neurotic."[5] Management's problem was to find ways to
exclude the compulsive or nonconforming programmer
whose behavior could not be predicted or shaped for
increased productivity. It was also a matter of weeding out
workers whose behavior had created "culture shock" within
the corporate structure.[6] Programmers more than operators
posed this management dilemma because the nature of their
work was harder to standardize and therefore left more
room for unpredictable behavior.

To select desirable programmers the hiring process relies
basically on the Programmer Aptitude Test (PAT).[7] Its
function is to find "logical abilities" through a series of
mathematical, verbal, and graphic problems. Both data-
processing managers and personnel managers agree that it
alone provides insufficient criteria for hiring. But like most
aptitude tests, it does serve as a funnel in the selection
process, favoring successful test-takers over those whose
fears or lack of schooling have prevented them from developing this skill.

In addition to the aptitude test, many companies give
standard personality profile "tests" to see if the applicant
will indeed fit the company mold. The personality tests, like
the PAT, are also measures of "test sophistication." As

Gerald Weinberg points out smart test-takers will "cheat" to make their personalities fit the requirements:

> As we know, applicants for programming jobs are likely to be a rather clever bunch, so we can assume that a great deal of "cheating" will take place if they are given such tests. But that should not worry us, for if they cheat successfully they are probably going to have a number of the critical personality traits we desire—*adaptability* to sense the direction of the test, ability to tolerate the stress of being examined by someone they don't know under *assumptions they cannot challenge, assertiveness* to do something about it, and *sense of humor* enough to enjoy the challenge.[8]

Weinberg argues that we are more likely to make a personality mistake in hiring a programmer than an intelligence mistake," because preselection criteria such as college degrees usually take care of the latter. He provides a long list of personality traits to be looked for in the "good" or "professional" programmer, including tolerance of stress, adaptability to change, neatness, humility, assertiveness, and the strong need for a sense of humor![9] As in most corporate hiring, a series of in-depth interviews are also required. The larger the company the longer the process, as the applicant weaves his or her way from the personnel department to the first-line data-processing managers. Usually the emphasis is on the ability of the applicant to be well-groomed, articulate, and poised rather than on technical proficiency.

Despite the use of standard personnel selection practices, the most consistent predictor of on-the-job success seems to be prior experience. Mayer and Stalnaker, for example, studied the influence of such factors as age, college major field, parental education, and interests, and found that none had as strong a prediction probability as prior experience.[10] Internal or in-house recruiting has often been favored for this reason. Not only does it give the company the chance to use someone whose personality traits are known, it also bolsters the corporate image, for it gives workers whose jobs are endangered by data processing the opportunity to retrain in the new field. Banks have been particularly successful with internal recruiting methods, although most data-processing workers are usually hired from outside the corporate walls.[11] In-house recruits are expected to pass the Programmer Aptitude Test, but in many instances the college degree requirement is waived.

By the late 1960s, job fragmentation, specialization, and standardization had progressed to the point where different selection criteria were used for different job definitions. In-house recruiting, for example, was often used to find people for the lower level coding functions. A programmer in a large bank comments on the difference between in-house and college recruitment procedures:

> Generally the people who were selected for retraining within the company were a little older and came from working-class backgrounds. Usually they didn't have a college degree. In programming they were assigned to applications maintenance work, you know, the real repetitive stuff.
>
> The college kids who were recruited directly from the outside were usually right out of college. They came from more middle-class families. These kids were assigned to the newer applications and the more exciting "state of the art" work.

The four-year bachelor's degree is required for the less routine applications and systems programming jobs, and the two-year associate degree is accepted for the lower level routine applications such as maintenance of existing programs.

The type of degree required and the specific characteristics of the selection process are highly dependent on the conditions in the labor market. During the first half of the 1970s the depressed economy virtually eliminated the corporate recruitment procedure for data-processing workers. Companies that did need to increase their programming staff were able to pick and choose from the large selection of already trained programmers in the labor market. Now, with the expansion of data-processing uses and therefore jobs, the issue of recruitment of new programmers has been reawakened. The issues of both aptitude-testing and college requirements are again being debated. Jack Stone, who writes a trade column called "The Human Connection," comments on the aptitude tests: "Aptitude testing for entry-level DPers is currently under fire because of concerns that such tests are inherently biased toward certain social classes and therefore are not sufficiently accurate in predicting successful performance in the DP environment."[12] In a sense, the issue is even more complicated now than it was in the sixties, for corporations still perceive a need to select the personality and technical requirements that best fit their needs *and* at the same time meet government affirmative action policies. The combination of aptitude tests, degree requirements, and corporate personality profiles tends to close the doors to minority groups.

Although the selection criteria are continually debated, they have clearly been successful in changing the characteristics of programmers and weeding out the misfits. The behavior traits that Richard Edwards calls "rules orientation," "habits of predictability and dependability," and "internalization of the enterprises's goals and values" are emphasized in the selection process.[13] Rather than seeking workers whose primary characteristic is their ability to solve complex problems, companies look for behavior traits that fit their style.

Education

In his discussions about the "knowledge" worker, Drucker argues that the most important element in increasing the worker's productivity is the need for formal education: "The greatest obstacle to economic growth . . . [is] the craft organization of work . . . which puts tremendous premium on doing things the way they used to be done."[14]

He sees formal systematized education as a way of breaking the bonds of apprenticeship, or informal training.

The call for data-processing education, like the call for work standards, was a familiar management theme in the 1960s. Whereas individual college-level courses in data-processing began to appear in the early sixties, formal computer science degree programs did not begin until late in the decade. Throughout this period, data-processing workers were educated by their on-the-job experience and training classes run by the company or computer manufacturer. Generally, programmers and operators were not expected to have any prior data-processing skills for employment. Once hired, they were put through an in-house training program or sent to "IBM school":

> Although IBM was not the first to manufacture large-scale, general purpose computers for commercial use, . . . they were the first to fully appreciate the wider social role of the programmer. It was that early insight which still accounts for the company's domination of the present-day general purpose machine market. Their training courses, even by the standards of the electrical industry upon whose traditions they drew, were elaborate and carefully done. So prestigious was training acquired at "IBM school," during the 1950s and early 1960s, that government and private employers used the lure of IBM training to recruit potential employees in what was then a tight seller's market in programming.[15]

Typically, the programmer course was six weeks long, with one week devoted to the fundamentals of computer hardware and five weeks on programming languages.

Operators were sent to IBM classes and given in-house training, but usually their instruction was shorter and more oriented toward "hands-on" learning. Both programmers and operators were expected to learn from the traditional craft "buddy" system. Workers were placed in groups with more experienced employees to ask questions and follow their actions. Generally, "buddies" were very cooperative and took the time, whenever possible, to fill the gaps in knowledge. But the results were uneven. During periods of great pressure and crisis (a "standard operating procedure" in data-processing operating and programming shops) experienced workers were unavailable and the novices were left to shift for themselves. In addition, the knowledge imparted by the experienced or "master" worker was, of course, the knowledge that the "master" wanted to transfer. It still remained out of management hands.

In an attempt to reduce the costs and increase the standardization of training, management introduced pro-grammed instruction manuals (PI's) in the early 1960s. Encouraged by IBM, PI texts allowed operators and programmers to learn at their own pace and when time allowed. Advocates of this approach argued that they replaced "master/novice pairing" with a controllable set of information that could be used with large numbers of workers.[16] PI's are still in fairly widespread use today for both programming and operations. They have also been updated to include computer-aided-instruction (CAI) and programmed film-loops, which instruct and test the work-ers in the basics of their trade.[17]

Another form of privately organized training was the technical trade school, which appeared in increasing numbers during the 1960s. Technical schools primarily trained people for operations positions, although some did specialize in programmer training. Their matchbook, radio, and TV advertisements were aimed at attracting working-class youth. They usually offered part-time programs of six months to one year, which stressed the technical details of running equipment (almost always IBM hardware) or programming languages. Although cries were heard from industry spokesmen about dishonest trade schools, they were, by and large, tolerated by most companies because they provided a supply of trained personnel. A 1972 study of the industry found that only 25 per cent of the companies surveyed hired EDP-school graduates in programming, but in general they were pleased with the quality of the education.[18] In many cases students studied programming, but were hired for operations because they lacked the college degree.

The military represented another important source of technical training, particularly for operations and technician positions. In fact, most computer technicians (those who repair the hardware) and many computer operators were hired directly after their military training ended. The large number of men in these areas is sometimes attributed to their prior military experience.

Although these forms of training remained adequate for operations positions, it was felt that they did not provide enough of the desired characteristics for programming jobs. Managers argued that it took programmers two years of on-the-job experience to be considered "productive." The demand for programmers in the 1960s was so high they could jump to another job for more pay by the end of their training period. The burden of education was felt to be an expensive one for the corporation. In addition, there was no way to insure that on-the-job knowledge would meet the standards of increasingly rationalized procedures. By the late 1960s, programming was solidly entrenched as a "profession," and as such it required academic credentials.

In 1968 the bachelor's degree in computer science was introduced and such major schools as New York University and Purdue began to offer programs. Much industry and academic debate followed, as to what the degree would involve. In some colleges it grew out of the mathematics department and therefore concentrated in the area of scientific problems; in others, it developed from the engineering curriculum and tended to follow the technical base. While academics debated its content, managers in industry were unified in their demands for emphasis on standards and discipline as well as technical detail.[19]

Most bachelor's programs in computer science concentrate on the study of computer hardware and the theory behind operating system software. Their graduates qualify for programming positions, although as a rule they do not train in job-oriented programming languages. Many computer science students now go on to graduate study, but those that enter the job market provide a solid source of systems programmers and some sophisticated applications programmers. A programming manager in a large company summarized computer science students by saying, "They can't code under pressure worth a damn, but at least we know what to *expect* from them."

An increasing number of business applications programmers and systems analysts come from bachelor's programs in business administration, which now offer at least some courses in programming and information-processing. This trend was first noted in a 1966 study of programmer vocational interests, which showed that business administration was second to mathematics in degrees held by programmers.[20]

By the 1970s, colleges had assumed the training of data-processing workers with programs designed to meet management objectives for discipline and structured knowledge. But to many managers, the educational process has gone too far in producing a sense of discipline. One manager, for example, commented, "It is the computer science degree that is the biggest offender in regimenting thinking—it produces plodders instead of thinkers." Another manager complained that he has great difficulty getting these well-disciplined graduates to think and act on their own: "Sure, they are disciplined and educated, but the educational process only trains them to think a certain way. They are trained to be systematic, but they don't know how to act in a crisis."

Neither the computer science nor the business administration degrees provided the type of education needed for the increasing number of lower-level program-coding jobs. When IBM and the other computer manufacturers began charging for programming training courses, it became clear that another source of pretrained programmers had to be found.[21] That source has been the two-year community college, conferring an Associate of Applied Science degree that emphasizes the programming and job-oriented training not included in the bachelor's degree. In the late 1970s some community colleges have begun to expand their curriculum and offer the associate degree with a major in computer operations.

As a teacher in a community college program, I am aware that the program offers good skills-oriented training, but that this training used to be provided by the companies themselves. Although the training function and expense have shifted from corporations to the academic community and the community at large, the purpose still remains very much under corporate control. Any community college that does not turn out job-ready workers will fail to attract students. In today's college market, colleges cannot afford to ignore industry. The Association for Computing Machinery has published guidelines for community college curricula. They urge that "in addition to being skilled technically as a computer programmer, [the graduate] must be able to use communications skills and related talents to work in an organization responsibly, effectively, and productively."[22] The newly added emphasis on organizational responsibility had always been *assumed* in college programs, but rarely stated explicitly. An employer commented on industry's need for these "skills": "In the old days, when you hired a college graduate, you at least knew that they would probably fit in to the company—now, you have to 'teach' them how to behave. The schools obviously should do this for us, because it's too expensive for us to do ourselves."

Motivation

From a management perspective, good selection and education procedures lessen the gap between the purchased labor-power and the labor actually applied on the job. Motivation on the job attempts to further reinforce characteristics desired by management. The literature of management science contains a large supply of tools to help managers motivate workers. Three of the most important techniques in governing workers' daily activities are job ladders, performance evaluation, and the ideology of professionalism. All three focus on *impersonal* methods for motivating workers. They are the mechanisms of bureaucratic organization that rely on the rules embedded in the structure rather than left to the arbitrary or whimsical power of the "boss."[23] At the root of all motivational policy, however, is the foundation of simple authority on which the policy rests. Although it may be masked behind a depersonalized and seemingly impartial set of procedures, managerial authority is the power to fire or at least transfer the worker who does not perform according to the rules.

Job ladders, or hierarchies, appear as natural to workers today as the division of labor that preceded them, but their function often has nothing to do with fragmented or specialized duties. Indeed, as Brecher and Costello explain, ladders are used to increase control of the work force: "On most jobs, workers are stratified into a number of different job categories and pay grades. At first sight, these may appear to result directly from the nature of the various functions to be performed. But in reality they are one more weapon in the employer's arsenal of control."[24] Job ladders are common to almost all bureaucratic organizations. Also called "training ladders," they typically include several steps or levels for each job category. In data processing, for example, separate ladders are maintained for programmers, systems analysts, and computer operators. A programming ladder might consist of titles such as programmer trainee, junior programmer, programmer, lead programmer, and programmer analyst.

To the worker, job ladders offer concrete evidence of company rules and procedures. Since job ladders are usually attached to formal standards and job definitions, they help make the future more explicit and possibly more secure. In addition, they lend credence to the concept of "career" versus "just a job." Workers caught up in the anonymity of large corporations are often pleased with the prospect of promotional ladders because they formally establish the possibility of a future. As one worker explains, the existence of codified job steps gives him something to look forward to—and an established way of getting there: "I was doing the job of a Lead Operator long before they made me one. I finally got the promotion because I could point to the job description book and say—'Look, that's what I do already.' They couldn't argue with the facts, they had to promote me."

Although workers may rely on the formal procedures that job ladders enforce, they also know that the ladders themselves are often a fiction, used to give a sense of mobility to an otherwise stationary situation. A systems analyst describes the situation in his company: "Every month the personnel department hassles us for job descriptions and possible changes in our title structure; they want it all down on paper. We produce these job descriptions but they are a fiction. They're bullshit to us—our department never really uses them, but top management wants them."

Because data-processing departments were late additions to existing corporate structures, their job ladders often contain extra steps to reflect the corporate standards.[25] This makes the notion of "promotion" even more ludicrous as the differences between job descriptions are often infinitesimal. In many cases there may only be the difference between two words; for example, a programmer trainee may work under *close* supervision and a junior programmer under supervision.[26] The proliferation of job titles allows managers to use them as they see fit:

> The titles make it easier for me to reward someone who has done really well, or to deny someone a promotion because they haven't done what I want them to.

> Lots of times programmers at different levels will be writing programs at the same level of complexity. To me the titles are a way of telling people what I expect of them.

Although standard management literature claims that ladders are a necessary reflection of the complexity of work, few line managers or workers accept the claim.

Thus, although ladders may be used to give workers a

sense of mobility, they are also used to keep people in place. Kraft spells this out for programming positions: "Ironically, the proliferation of slightly different job titles and descriptions has come about when there are fewer rather than more real opportunities for career advancement."[27]

In most firms no automatic procedure allows for crossing from one ladder to another. Computer operators, for example, are not necessarily welcomed into the programming ranks, no matter how well they may do on the job. Similarly, programmers may not automatically transfer to systems titles after they have climbed the programming hierarchy. Although some companies allow this type of mobility, for the most part job ladders within each category are treated as isolated structures. The most noticeable effect of separate and unequal hierarchies is the existence of discrimination. With different methods of selection and degrees of education being used for entry into each ladder, it is not surprising that the ladders reflect a stratified set of social relations. Various studies of the data-processing field have found that discrimination by sex, race, ethnic group, and age exists between and within ladder categories.[28] In general, computer operators are men, and the set-up and support functions are performed by women. Both kinds of operations titles—operators and the more clerical input/ output support functions—are filled by recruitment procedures that usually draw young working-class people, often from immigrant and minority populations. Applications programming titles are divided by rungs within the ladder. Today the lower rungs within the applications ladders are increasingly being filled by women; the higher one goes up the ladder, the more the positions are held by college-educated males. Systems programmers, the "elite" among programming ranks, are most often men from middle-class and professional families. Systems analysts generally are selected from the same backgrounds.

The divisions found in data-processing clearly reflect those of the larger society. Job ladders reinforce them by keeping workers "locked" into separate paths. In addition to keeping workers apart, these structures foster competition and antagonism among groups. Job ladders exacerbate the feud between systems analysts, programmers, and operators. Selected from different environments, educated in different characteristics, and motivated by different mechanisms, the groups become increasingly isolated. Fifteen years ago data-processing workers created "culture shock" for the firm. In response they tended to draw together and unify themselves against the rest of the company.[29] But that was before division of labor had been formally established through job ladders. Today, it is more likely that data-processing workers will keep the feud within the data-processing family. They are consequently less likely to challenge management or interfere with the rest of the company.

Performance evaluations supplement the motivational effects of the job ladders. The two are closely tied together. Managers use periodic performance reviews to grant or deny promotions. Although management literature outlines the ways evaluation sessions can be used to help improve the worker's performance, it is most generally agreed that their primary function is to reinforce the system of reward and punishment.[30]

Data-processing workers have come to expect semi-annual or annual appraisals of their work. Performance evaluation is usually a standardized procedure whereby the worker is given a report, orally and/or in writing, about his or her performance on the job. At IBM, for example, the appraisal system consists of a long checklist of evaluation criteria, very much like a grade school report card. The criteria include such categories as appearance, conduct, tardiness, and overall presentation, as well as technical proficiency. Since performance evaluation almost always includes these behavioral categories, it is also known as "trait-raiting." Trait-rating systematizes weeding out of workers with "inappropriate" behavior traits. Like the other mechanisms of behavioral control, it operates within a depersonalized structure.

As a motivational strategy, performance evaluation is usually tied to salary as well as job title. An "excellent" rating, for example, may gain the worker a 6 to 8 per cent salary increase, depending, of course, on the general market conditions. Many companies use a procedure that requires the worker to get two "excellent" or "superior" grades before promotion can be considered. Performance evaluation or formal trait-rating is generally accepted by most workers in the same way that the job ladders are. Although they recognize that the standards can be used against them, workers hope that the impersonal nature of the appraisals will give them security.

To a certain extent trait-rating is successful in channeling workers who accept corporate behavioral rules. Generally, the higher levels of the corporate career ladder hold managers with more pronounced traits of "internalization of company goals" and "habits of dependability and predictability." In his study of corporate leadership, Michael Maccoby paints a new breed of people who are moving into higher levels in the corporate structure:

> The modern gamesman is best defined as a person who loves change and wants to influence its course. He likes to take calculated risks and is fascinated by techniques and new methods. He sees a developing project, human relations, and his own career in terms of options and possibilities, as if they were a game. . . . He is cooperative but competitive, detached and playful, but compulsively driven to succeed; a team player but a would-be superstar; a team leader but often a rebel against bureaucratic hierarchy.[31]

The description is applicable to the men who rise up data-processing ladders and land on management rungs. The right blend of cooperation and competition, the ability to take calculated risks, and the assessment of options are all part of the demands of management science. Management science stresses the necessity to quantify variables and then find the right mix to "solve" a problem. In the attitudes of the men (and the few women) who climb the ladders, being able to find the right mix is instilled as carefully as the rules in a game. Subcultures that do not reinforce these values, with their gamelike rules and rewards, do not get to climb the ladder, and some are not even allowed in the game. Performance evaluation reinforces the choices.

Ironically, by removing the arbitrary nature of lower management jobs, performance evaluation standards also remove a good deal of lower management power. They not only allow line managers to observe workers closely, they also let top managers keep tabs on lower and middle managers. As standards and formal procedures are pushed farther up the job ladder, it becomes increasingly important for management to encourage workers to concentrate on higher goals rather than on dissatisfactions within their current environment. By routinizing the decision-making process, performance evaluations raise the same problems for managers they do for workers, especially when the latter are "professionals."

Professionalism is an ideological conception implying that workers control entry into their profession, set their own standards, and have a loyalty or duty to the public. Clearly, these characteristics do not apply to data-processing workers: they are first and foremost corporate employees who perform tasks at the direction of their employers. This is true for all titles within the data-processing hierarchy. Management has promoted professionalism as a motivational technique. The technique implies that the "professional" employee should feel obligated to get the work done, usually with little supervision. One data-processing worker put it this way: "Becoming a 'professional' means that we have to get all the work done and not get paid overtime for the hours we put in." In corporate jargon, professionalism has come to be a catchword meaning that workers should "act appropriately" and do whatever is expected.[32]

Professionalism is also used to separate workers. Most companies maintain a distinction between "professional" workers, who are salaried, and "nonprofessional" employees, working "on the clock" (for hourly wages). Usually workers from the operations ladder through the lower programming ladders (coders) are considered nonprofessional. The 1971 Department of Labor decision that ruled programmers out of the professional ranks technically left only systems analysts in the professional arena. But managers and data-processing associations continue to push the image of professionalism as a form of internal regulation. An officer of the Association of Computer Programmers and Analysts and of the Institute for Certification of Computer Professionals complained that the professional societies are "carrying the banner" for professionalism in the face of "rank and file" lack of interest.[33]

The issue of professionalism is being kept very much alive today by plans to push voluntary certification of programmers, systems analysts, and data-processing managers. The Institute for Certification of Computer Professionals (ICCP), which administers the examination for Certificate in Data Processing (CDP), has argued that the "CDP is the most important certificate program to recognize expertise and professional attitude."[34] While the CDP has begun to gain wider acceptance, it is usually recognized as a form of individual accomplishment rather than formal authority. The certificate program helps managers to remind workers about their "professional" duties, and at the same time it insures that a given body of technical knowledge is maintained under the control of industry management.

Professionalism seems to have been successful in keeping unions out of programming and systems job categories. Until the 1970s most large unions did not even attempt to organize programmers, although inroads were made in organizing operations workers. Now, unions such as the Office and Professional Employees International (OPEIU) and the Communications Workers of America (CWA) are becomming active in seeking data-processing workers. Organizers argue that data-processing work is like other work because the workers "can't name their own price any more. Some are even being laid off. They're worried about job security, arbitrary assignment of bad shifts, fringe benefits, but most of all they're concerned about money."[35]

So far, union organizing among programmers has been

slow and strikes have been few. In two strikes that included data-processing workers, one among San Francisco municipal employees, the other at Blue Cross in New York, the data-processing installations were kept going by management.[36] A programmer who had been involved in attempts during the early 1970s to start a union commented on this problem:

> Ten years ago we thought that if we could get a union together we would have had total power in a strike. Imagine shutting down an entire DP center— why that would impact the whole company! Management would have never been able to do anything about it because they didn't know anything about data processing.

Organizing efforts have also been slowed by the split between "professionals" and "nonprofessionals." In one case, workers in an insurance company tried to organize, but negotiations broke down when it was suggested that programmers and operators be included in the same bargaining unit. Although the Labor Department no longer considers programmers to be professional employees, they are reluctant to accept the new image.[37] As skill and decision-making are removed from programming jobs, the image of professionalism offers a sense of status. The status, in turn, increases division and competition among workers.

Of course, many managers in the field feel that job ladders, ratings, and pseudo-professionalism are not the best ways to motivate data-processing employees. Additionally, they believe that the selection and education procedures should be less strongly oriented to the corporate norm. Humanistic managers argue that these mechanisms have become obstacles to motivating workers on a personal one-to-one level. They feel that workers are more interested in job-related rewards, such as more challenging tasks, than in corporate rewards such as promotion. Debate between the two schools has dominated trade literature and shop-floor discussion. The poles of the arguments are probably best expressed in an allegorical story by Miles Benson.

Benson outlines a plot in which a group of "assembly-line" programmers are pitted against a group of "craftsmen" for a "code-off contest," the idea being to decide, once and for all, which approach produces the best programs. He describes the dichotomy between the two worlds:

> Over at Alchemy [the assembly-line shop], Stan Sorcerer runs a tight ship. His employees have a dress code, fixed working hours, specified coffee breaks, and a strict behavior program.

> The standards defined for his programmers are profuse and rigid. Management of tasks is by schedule, and if a programmer gets behind in his work he is expected to put in voluntary overtime to make it up. The atmosphere is tense, businesslike, and productive. Stan is fond of quoting data which show his programmers produce three times the national average.

> Stan Sorcerer has built himself a software factory, and he runs his shop like an assembly-line.

> But at Softli Paper, the craft shop, Herb Bond sees things differently. Herb's programmers' dress could best be described as neo-hippy. They come and go through the swinging doors of Softli at all hours of the day or night.

> The standards manual would fit within the index of that used at Alchemy. . . . Herb uses peer code reviews, but never conducts management code inspections.

> Management of tasks is by progress reporting, with emphasis on product quality rather than schedule.

Benson's point is that there is no clearly proven superior method—yet. The "craftsmen" and the "assembly-liners" both still have room to operate because "the Henry Ford of software hasn't come forth yet":

> The results of the code-off, in case you're waiting

with baited breath, were an anti-climax. Scoring anomalies aside, it was a standoff. The Alchemy Assembly Liners had an easier time with the report generator [the standardized program] and did well in time and cost factors.

But Softli Craftmen did better with the precomplier [a more complex program], and their quality scores were higher.[38]

It is probably true that there is not yet *one* proven method for increasing worker productivity; it is also clear that the strategies for selecting, educating and motivating data-processing workers have proven effective in producing workers whose behavior is more controllable. Of the two types of managerial efficiency discerned by David Gordon—greater output and increased control over workers—data-processing management seemed to feel that this second form was necessary before the increased quantitative efficiency could be effectively tackled.[39] It appears that the majority of data-processing shops have adopted the strategies described in this chapter.

The methods of social control, particularly those used in the selection and education process, are quite pervasive. It is difficult for workers individually to fight against them. Although data-processing workers reacted against the standards and rules imposed on the work process, they were less successful in changing the mechanisms that directly affected their behavior on the job. As we shall see in Chapter 8, however, although they have adapted to the job-related characteristics demanded by corporate norms, they do not necessarily agree with them.

The argument that data-processing workers were in short supply was really an additional excuse for formalizing the mechanisms of behavior control. In a field short of specialists, there certainly has been a great deal of selectivity in choosing from this "supply." Indeed, the selection process appears to be more a means to weed out potential disrupters than a method to select people with the right technical characteristics.[40] Selection and education criteria help management control the supply of workers in the labor *market*. Motivation techniques assist management in their control of the labor *process* on the job.

Selecting, educating, and motivating data-processing workers are problems of both cost (efficiency) and behavioral objectives (social control). In terms of cost, a poor selection of workers can result in high training and turnover expenses, as well as the incredible cost of potential sabotage. In terms of behavior, an improper choice of workers can result in behavioral problems causing unpredictable performance and "culture shock." The *safest* management practice seems to require merging objectives. The "predictable performer" may not always be the most creative or the most productive, but at least his or her behavior fits within the predetermined guidelines of bureaucratic structure. It allows production to continue at a steady, if sometimes slower, pace. But what is probably most outstanding about corporate techniques of social control is that they *channel workers not to fight back*. They can be given a sense of security, status, and promotion without changing the existing power structure.

The message in Benson's story poses another set of contradictions for management. The more workers are compressed into controllable behavior patterns the more they lose the interest (and sometimes the ability) to think and act for themselves. In the 1960s data-processing management was concerned about rebellious workers; today it complains about lack of interest and incentive on the part of workers.[41]

CHAPTER
6

Management Organization

Workers are told that managerial authority and responsibility are necessary to coordinate work tasks. But Jeremy Brecher and Tim Costello offer another interpretation: "In fact, managerial authority over work developed not because workers were *unable* to direct their work themselves, but rather to prevent them from doing so."[1] Management theory presents managerial authority and its modern counterpart, bureaucratic organization structure, as a series of principles mandated by the size, complexity, and technology of corporate functions. Yet when we look at the work being done at the bottom of the organization hierarchy, we find that, wherever possible, it is done cooperatively, often disregarding management principles. Certainly the work is divided, but its division does not necessarily match the rules established by management authority. In data processing, we often find that the more complicated the project the more collective the activities, although management theory argues that complicated tasks require more division of labor. First-line managers and supervisors are well aware of this difference between management theory and practice. They may know that worker *productivity is dependent on cooperative actions* rather than bureaucratic procedures, but they must enforce the rules handed down to them through the hierarchy.

Many workers blame the encroachment of bureaucratic procedures on stupid or incompetent managers. Trade journals and management consultants call conflicts between the two forms of relationships "mismanagement." But it seems unlikely that bureaucratic procedures would have conquered as much data-processing territory as they have if they were simply a case of mismanagement. I argue, as does Richard Edwards in his writings on bureaucratic control, that the bureaucratic structure has taken over because it carefully balances measurable worker productivity and an ability to keep people in their place.[2]

Hierarchy and Bureaucracy

As the organization of data-processing activities has parallelled that of its parent firms, it has become more bureaucratic as well as more rationalized. The more rationalized the structure the more circumscribed the activities of the workers. Richard H. Hall describes how work is shaped: "It is through the organizationally defined routinization of tasks, formalization and standardization of rules and procedures, centralization or decentralization of power and emphasis on hierarchical distinctions that work is presented to the worker."[3] Organizational structure reflects both the way that work is done and the characteristics of the workers. As the work process is rationalized and the characteristics of the workers are shaped by management to fit corporate standards, the organizational structure within which these take place also becomes rationalized. Work is a social activity, but the arrangement of this activity is determined by management needs for coordination and control. Data processing, in particular, is a collective activity. Workers are organized into task- or project-oriented teams, and these teams are linked into data-processing departments. Rationalization of this structure has meant that people and information can be confined within predictable places and actions.

On the surface, the rationalization of organization structure appears to allow greater objectivity and a sense of order. Clearly defined organization charts capture formal chains of command. Higher management can call on the chart for an instant accounting of who is responsible for "failure" or "success." Middle and lower managers know what and *who* they are responsible for and where the limits of their authority end. Workers get a clear picture of where they fit in and where they can climb to. Yet this "rational" order expresses a series of power relations that confine movement and contradict concepts such as freedom and democracy. These power relations pose contradictions that are continually pushing carefully balanced organization schemes into new formations and unraveling the objectivity and "rationality" of the formal structure. They reveal that the hierarchical order of modern business is not as "natural" as most would like to believe.

Management theory supports the concept of hierarchical order, based on three basic assumptions. The first asserts that hierarchical formations are found in society and nature, therefore they are treated as "given." The second argues that once labor has been divided it must be put back together again, and this putting-together process involves direction by management. The third, which applies most directly to data processing, holds that the size, complexity, and technology of modern business require extensive division and coordination of labor. All three assumptions provide a justification for management actions, but shed little light on why labor is divided and reformed into the *specific* rationalized power relations that appear in corporate structure today.[4] Nor do they tell us why data-processing structure has copied these forms of organization. Like Humpty-Dumpty, many companies find themselves in situations where the tasks of putting together the divided work cannot be done—even with the help of all the corporate men.

Typically, changes in organizational structure rate a collective shrug from the workers involved, yet management theory and practice spend a great deal of time defining and defending these changes. If hierarchical structure were as natural and necessary as the basic assumptions would have us believe, then what contradictions produce the radically different informal work networks? And why does the formal structure, even when applied to new areas such as data processing, continue to be more stratified in the face of conflicting worker interests?

Hierarchy allows directives to be carried down a chain of command along with procedures for enforcing the directives. The more successful the structure the more clearly orders are communicated and acted upon.[5] In theory, directives carried to the lowest level have the same degree of successful implementation as those that go down only a notch or two. What is most remarkable about this funneling idea is that directives can flow only down, not *up*. Information can flow from management to workers with ease; only selected communication can flow from workers to managers. And the information that flows back up the hierarchy is often distorted. Take, for example, the case of project deadlines:

> As a programmer I know about when my program will be finished, and if I need more time to get it done. But I'm not directly asked these questions. Instead I have to fill out zillions of forms which specify the information they want—like percent of completion in coding, or percent of test data design. They get this information, but they don't really know what I'm doing.

In directing the flow of information, hierarchy *retards* change that could be initiated by workers, but hastens change stemming from management. We may be taught to take hierarchical control for granted because we see it in family, school, and social structures, but that does not explain its function. It is so much a part of our social fabric that there is little wonder that workers shrug and go on creating their own informal networks.

The central contradiction, then, is that change can come only from the managers to the managed. Workers may be "plugged" into the structure, but their needs do not always fit. Even job enrichment schemes and human relations programs, while attempting to reorganize work processes, do not tamper with the basic hierarchy of power relations. Besides developing their own informal networks, workers resist with methods that range from "gripe" sessions to sabotage.

Worker response produces contradictions between *co-ordinating* divided labor processes and *controlling* workers to do the work. Not only must management see to it that the divided work is put back together (coordinated), but managers are also increasingly charged with controlling workers as if they were as interchangeable as the work processes. Workers who control or keep knowledge in their heads make it difficult for managers to exercise authority. In moving toward a more "rational" structure, organizations have attempted to place coordination and control *higher* in the managerial hierarchy. In other words, the essence of managerial power is moved farther away from the reach of worker reaction. The more rationalized the structure, the more standard and routine become the functions of lower to middle managers.[6] Edwards calls this bureaucratic control, emphasizing that control becomes "institutionalized by vesting it in official positions or roles and permitting its exercise only according to prescribed rules, procedures and expectations."[7]

Hierarchical organization in data processing suffers from the same problems that plague the structure in general. Managerial attempts to find solutions to these problems have resulted in constantly changing structures. Each attempt to reshape the management superstructure has made it, like the work process, more rationalized and less intuitive.

Worker response also creates conflicts between formal management structure and their own informal patterns. Sociologists tell us that most businesses have two structures—the formal and the informal.[8] The formal structure carefully defines roles and inserts people into those roles. It is represented by the organization chart that shows how work and communication are divided among workers and coordinated by management. The informal structure is usually quite different. Within it, workers and in many cases managers communicate and interact in ways not etched on the organization chart. In his study of data-processing departments, Marshall Meyer found that informal networks were tolerated so long as they did not interfere with the objectives of the firm.[9] In the data-processing area, the most noticeable difference is that the larger 'and more complex the work becomes, the more workers tend to share their knowledge *collectively*, replacing formal divisions with informal cooperation.

Among data-processing workers this split between formal organization and informal practice is often talked about. A systems analyst summarized it this way:

> They [top management] keep changing the organization chart. The name of the game is change the structure. We've come to accept yearly restructuring—they just keep shuffling managers around. At least once a year there is some major productivity crisis and their response is to reorganize us into different groups and make the groups report to different managerial functions.

> We've come to take these changes as commonplace. Sometimes we don't even talk about it; we just go on doing what we always do.

Data processing may have fallen into the web of bureaucratic organization, but it still presents problems in terms of its "professional" activities. Peter Blau, for example, notes that bureaucratic authority conflicts with professional authority, causing problems for workers with technical skills. He finds that the conflicts arise because bureaucratic authority, which rests on power vested in the structure, "obligates subordinates to follow directives under threat of sanctions," whereas professional authority, like craft work, requires expertise and *self-government* of individuals and groups.[10] This is precisely the problem data-processing managers face. Workers such as higher level programmers and systems analysts, who control knowledge, consider themselves professional and are stifled by bureaucratic structure. Additionally they do not respond well to the discipline imbedded in the structure. Drucker argues that the "knowledge worker" should not be stuck in a standard hierarchy: "The basic capital resource [sic] . . . is the knowledge worker who puts to work what he has learned in systematic education."[11] He feels that managers in knowledge-based industry should be leery of division of labor and its subsequent integration into bureaucratic structure, because it "divorce[s] planning from doing," failing to make knowledge productive.[12]

Both Drucker and Blau notice that as knowledge-based industry becomes more bureaucratic, worker resistance and informal structure grow. They have written extensively about the dangers of bureaucratic organization, yet despite their well-known reputations their warnings have gone unheeded by management. Rather than adapting the organization to fit the knowledge worker, managers have continued on the path of adjusting the worker and the work process to fit bureaucratic control.

Periodically, industries go through times of transition when bureaucratic structure does conflict with professional and therefore unrationalized work activities. Such is the case in the data-processing field. Programming and systems analysis are in a state of transition. As professional work processes and attitudes clash with the bureaucratic structure of the larger firm, management finds it difficult to increase worker productivity. Bureaucratic structure seems to be more effective for such activities as operations, which have passed through the transition stage and have become more fully rationalized. What Drucker and Blau fail to see is the tendency for the "knowledge" or professional worker to be "odd person out." The management structure will not be changed to fit him or her; the worker is being changed to fit the structure. In data processing, as in other knowledge-based occupations such as engineering, it is the number of rationalized jobs that is growing, not the number of professional jobs.[13]

Data-Processing Organization

In rationalized data-processing work, the activities of operators are coordinated and controlled by the pace of the equipment and the software controls built into it. Operations work is task-oriented. In general, operators perform fairly well-defined tasks, which are observed by working supervisors. The supervisors can exercise only rigidly defined responsibility and authority. A shift supervisor describes the type of task he does in a medium-sized installation:

> I got four guys assigned to me on my shift. I try to rotate them so that they don't get too bored doing one thing all day. Like for example, I take somebody on the printer and put them on the tapes for a few hours.

> My job is to see that the production work which is scheduled [by a person with separate scheduling duties] gets done. I pitch in and operate as I'm needed. If anything goes wrong, or the system crashes [stops], I call in my boss, who calls the systems people.

Although operators develop their own informal communication networks, these do not generally conflict with the bureaucratic chain of command. Most decision-making has been removed from their routine tasks and incorporated either directly into the software (operating system) or into standard procedures that are easier for management to regulate. Since each task is coordinated and controlled by routinized procedures, there is little leeway for organizational problems. Like that of assembly-line workers, the operators' freedom to leave the machine room is limited by supervisory permission.

The nonroutine or developmental activities of pro-

gramming and analysis require far more managerial coordination and control. Almost without exception, programmers and systems analysts are hierarchically arranged
into teams that exist for the life of a project. Project life,
depending on its size, scope, and complexity, can range
from a few weeks to a decade.[14]

Most companies have three types of ongoing projects:
maintenance of existing programs, modification of existing
systems, and development of new ones. By far, the majority
of all work falls into the first two categories, which lend
themselves to more routine activities and therefore more
standard procedures. Maintenance work, which is the most
static, was described by a programmer:

> Maintenance is the pits. You know that when you
> are stuck doing this that you will never get out of it.
> All you do is fix programs that were already written
> by other people. In my shop we are even limited in
> the way we are allowed to fix bugs [errors] in
> programs. After a while it takes very little thought.
> At least it's more challenging when you get to do
> modifications, because you may get to write your
> own program or subroutine.

Modification projects often grow out of maintenance.
They may range from a few new programs to fit management requests for new reports to new subsystems to reflect
changes in management decision-making rules. In the
insurance business, for example, when new types of
insurance are added to the company line, computer
programs are added or modified to include the new policies.

Maintenance and, in some cases, modification tasks are
given to workers at the lowest level, and managed more in
the assembly-line style. Maintenance, in particular, can be
more clearly defined and controlled by bureaucratic forms
of management. The work is called "production" because
the programs are in constant use. Sometimes maintenance
crews have to be on call in case "bugs" develop in programs
that are needed by corporate management. This type of
work is done under high pressure: "I put in two years in a

production shop. I thought I was going to get an ulcer. I was the 'fix-it' man—they would call me day or night and even during vacations. And I never got to do anything really challenging."

The third type of project, development of new systems, involves the most nonroutine decision-making and therefore is the least rationalized. This is the area where professional work practices clash with bureaucratic corporate organization.

Projects reflect the functions and goals of the company. In banking, for example, there are separate projects for functions such as stock transfer, acceptances, trust accounts, and commercial loans. Today, the emphasis in most firms is on developing Management Information Systems, which attempt to link the files collected in each functional subsystem. These systems require large and often lengthy projects.

Project teams are structured around the technical and administrative needs of the function and do not necessarily involve people at all levels in the career ladder structure. A well-defined project, for example, may have a lead analyst and a string of low level coders. A complex subsystem may be made up of a senior analyst or manager and analyst-level programmers only. Climbing the career ladder does not usually change one's function within a project. In fact, to programmers trapped on long projects the rungs on the career ladder can mean very little; they just keep coding their segment of the assigned subsystem. Many times career ladder position and project duties do not even mesh:

> The best project I ever worked on was way back when I was a programmer analyst [the lowest level of analyst in that company]. I got to do a little of everything on the project, and I loved it. The people were great and the project lasted a little more than a year so I didn't get tired of it. I haven't enjoyed myself or been as challenged since.

For programmers and analysts the project team and its life-cycle are their work life. Team members have to work closely together. A group that functions well is usually one in which the people get along and have established their own communications networks and division of labor. A programmer for a large bank explained her relationship with a team working on a commercial loan system:

> I asked to be assigned to this particular team, not because I liked the application—I really hate accounting systems, and it involves a lot of program modification—but I like the people in the group.

> We had a closely knit group and everyone was very cooperative. Why, when I came in in the morning the others were already at work debugging my programs. We always shared our work and helped each other with sticky problems.

I found her experience to be the rule. Often, if given the choice, workers would place the social environment of the team before the technical details of the project.

Programmers and managers agree that the key to programming productivity is a team in which people enjoy one another and work cooperatively, a point on which Gerald Weinberg's book focuses.[15] But cooperative, often nonhierarchical, organization poses problems farther up the management hierarchy. Cooperative and flexible work organization does not lend itself to managerial coordination and control. Typically, for a programmer the problem sounds like this:

> My project leader [technical supervisor] thinks I'm doing a great job. My programs are coded properly and I get along well with the others in the group.

> Unfortunately, my manager [administrator] is angry at me because I have been late a lot—although the others usually cover for me. He doesn't know what I'm doing, but he's the one who has final say on evaluating me at review time.

Line managers, on the other hand, are responsible for seeing that the work gets done on time and within the budget parameters set by their "superiors." They see it differently:

> They [the programmers] just don't understand how
> hard it is to control a project with this many people.
> I am responsible for seeing to it that the work is
> brought in on target and for the agreed budget. For
> that to happen I have to make sure that everyone is
> doing their job. When they get together and coffee-
> klatch all day I don't know what is happening.

The transient nature of project life-cycles usually means
that workers report to a technical supervisor in charge of
their team as well as to an administrative supervisor or
manager who serves as a sort of "home base." Technical
leadership is usually taken by senior analysts or, in the case
of large projects, it may be coordinated by supervisory titles.
Administrative functions are controlled by managerial
ranks.[16]

Splits between coordination of technical functions and
control of administrative ones only intensify upper management's need to increase bureaucratic sanctions. As the
pressure is applied from top management to "shape those
workers up," middle and line managers have few options
but to tighten control through greater discipline. From a
management viewpoint, workers who dress, behave, and fill
in their time sheets correctly *appear* to lessen management
headaches even if they are not being more productive.

Particular problems are caused by long projects, which
workers are likely to leave before they have completed their
segment. In theory, the more interchangeable the job
segments and workers, the easier it is to get by when a
worker leaves. But as Weinberg points out, programmers
do not like to be treated interchangeably and will find many
ways to show their resentment.[17] Their anger, often in the
form of slow-downs, increases management's attempts at
discipline. A programmer describes his frustrations:

> The project is so large I feel like I'll never get off of it.
> I don't even know what the damn thing is supposed
> to do. I know that I could work a lot harder, but I
> don't care. I code an "acceptable" amount every day

and spend a lot of time looking at the ceiling. The people on my team do the same.

Frederick P. Brooks, Jr., known as the "father of the IBM System/360," has written a book wonderfully titled *The Mythical Man-Month*.[18] His thesis is that most projects get caught in the proverbial "tar pits" because they make the mistake of believing that men [*sic*] and months are interchangeable for estimating cost and time. He points out the classical dilemma of communication—the more behind schedule the project is the more people are added to get it done. For Brooks, and clearly to those of us who have been caught in this "tar pit," more people require more communication, which, of course, requires greater coordination and control.

Brooks believes that the communications problems are aggravated by traditional hierarchical structure. To avoid it he supports the idea of "chief programmer" teams put forward by Harlan Mills. Mills's model is based on the surgical team: there is to be only one surgeon—the chief programmer—and all others support this person as the medical team supports the surgeon. Chief-programmer team structure is a break from traditional team organization. In the traditional hierarchy, the system is broken down into individual programs or modules (units smaller than a program). Each program can then be given to a different programmer, with the programmer responsible for carrying that program through all stages in the project life-cycle (coding through testing). Groups of programs and modules are coordinated by higher level analysts and these in turn are fitted into still higher levels within the system.[19]

Chief programmer teams require a hierarchy of a different sort. The surgeon or chief has total say over all aspects of the system. The chief would design *and code* the whole operation from start to finish. Supporting this person would be an assistant, or "copilot," who stands by ready to step in if disaster strikes. Brooks calls this person the "alter ego" of the surgeon, the one who discusses all problems and is fully familiar with all code.

Of course, the project requires an administrator to handle money, space, and people problems. But under this structure, the surgeon has final say in these matters, the administrator merely handles them to get them out of the surgeon's hair. Other support functions are filled by people who serve as "editors" to document the project's functions, secretaries who handle correspondence, and a program clerk who maintains all technical records. The team is rounded out with other technicians who specialize in technical details required by the surgeon.

Chief programmer teams avoid the problems of co-ordination, control, and communication by eliminating most forms of communication and putting all power in one person. But, of course, this structure creates an array of other problems. Chief programmer teams represent the ultimate in division of labor and specialization. They are founded on the principle of interchangeability of people within each specific support function.

Brooks comes from the "humanistic" school. As a "people-firster" he states: "Organizations must be designed around the people available; not people fitted into pure theory organizations."[20] But he seems to fall into his own trap. His efforts to solve the communication problem lead him head-first into that of division of labor. He replaces horizontal division of labor by vertical division[21] in order to end up with interchangeable specialists. Vertical division (such as the chief teams) allows communication to be channeled from chief to subordinates or from chief to other chiefs. He insists that the guiding principle must be a "careful division of labor between architecture and im-plementation."[22] Admitting that this contains a hint of "aristocracy" rather than "democracy," he argues that it is necessary for the "integrity" of the finished product. His recommendations sound like Frederick Taylor's early management dictums: some people are paid to think, others to follow. Brooks puts it this way:

> The purpose of organization is to reduce the amount of communication and control necessary. . . . The

means by which communication is obviated are *division of labor* and *specialization of function*. The tree-like structure of organizations reflects the diminishing need for detailed communication when division and specialization of labor are applied.[23]

Most programmers that I talked to were skeptical about the use of chief programmer teams and other attempted changes in project team organization. Although they accept a certain amount of divided labor, they want to be able to organize their own informal methods for putting the labor together: "They [management] can't legislate organization, and they certainly can't control the ways we communicate with each other. On every project that I've worked on, we [the team members] have always evolved our own network and organization."

The data-processing department exists as a service function to the rest of the firm. Problems of coordination and control of projects and tasks are further complicated because the services provided are requested by other departments within the parent firm. The department must be organized so that requests flow in and services flow out with the minimum amount of friction with user departments. But, as all data-processing workers and managers know, friction between data processing and user departments is fairly common. According to standard management theory, conflicts between data processing and other departments can be lessened by making data processing into the mold of the other, older departments. While this has been happening to some degree, it has not been an easy process as there are still characteristics of the data-processing function that do not fit the bureaucratic pattern.

Central to this difficulty is the division between two really separate data-processing services, which in classical terms are called staff functions and line functions. Staff capacity means that data-processing workers act in an *advisory* role to corporate higher management. Usually this includes matters such as consulting about computer application to a business problem or developing a new management information system. Advisory functions are hard to define and therefore difficult to rationalize. On the other hand, line services are those where the data-processing shop *directly* produces services for the organization. Turning out periodic reports on company financial statistics, for example, is a line function. The shape of the data-processing organization and its place within the corporate hierarchy have changed over time as the number of routine functions have increased and become line production functions. Originally, the data-processing function provided consulting or staff services to the rest of the company. Until the mid-1960s this function was the predominant one and communication between data processing and corporate management was strained and unpredictable. As the computer hardware and software developed, so did the applications themselves. Increasing numbers of records and reports were transferred to the data-processing shop, representing to some degree a transfer of responsibility and authority to data-processing managers.

Generally, services produced in the line capacity are more easily integrated into the corporate hierarchy; that is, data-processing "products" such as standard reports or updated files are churned out with rationalized procedures, clearly defined job titles, and standards for worker performance. This type of work includes programmers and analysts assigned to maintenance or modification projects, as well as all operations personnel. Communications problems are usually minimized since most work requests flow from user-department management to data-processing managers with little decision-making involved.

The atmosphere of work done in the line capacity is that of the high-intensity "production shop." Workers and line managers complain that two laws dominate their work schedules: the first is Murphy's Law, which states that anything that can go wrong will do so; the second, commonly called GIGO, reminds workers that Garbage brought into the processing, in the form of erroneous data, will result in Garbage Out. Line workers are expected to produce computerized "products" much the way the Xerox service would be expected to produce multiple copies. They are given direct standardized orders and expected to follow the predetermined procedures to the "T."

Problems in requesting computer services have decreased for upper corporate management as the functions of the data-processing department have become more routine. The pressures on data-processing workers and their immediate supervisors, however, have grown proportionally. Supervisors and first-line managers get caught in the squeeze as their functions are increasingly routinized. The complaint expressed by an operations manager in a bank installation typified that of many line managers:

> Work gets turned over to Operations when it is documented and fully tested. After that, we're expected to process it like we were processing shirts in the laundry. Top management has set standards so that they think that we can push a button and out pops the report. They don't understand that a lot of work goes into producing even the routine requests.

The staff functions of data processing are, by their very nature, less precisely defined. Corporate policy has begun to set standards for requesting data-processing advice, but it is difficult to rationalize the process whereby it is given. If, for example, the legal department wants to know if their cases can be maintained on computerized files, they are dependent on the "expert" opinion of the analysts assigned to the project. As Marshall Meyer pointed out in his study of government data-processing departments, the insertion of extra levels within the data-processing hierarchy at least gives upper management the feeling that they are communicating at the "proper" level.[24] But, for the most part, corporate line management is still mystified by the staff capacity of data processing and therefore seeks ways to control it better. This problem is in no way unique to data processing.

In staff functions, the lack of routine decision-making presents itself as a challenge to the workers. Consulting work, even within the confines of large corporations, retains some of the aura of the earlier data-processing "craft." One systems analyst described it this way: "Each problem presented to us is like a totally new experience. I get to do much more of the work—from beginning to end of the project. I get a complete picture and can see how the pieces fit together. I love the feeling of solving a problem." Due to their nonrationalized nature, staff problems require far more communication between workers and between managers, which in turn, requires more coordination and control. Line functions are structured to decrease problems of coordination and disciplinary control, but staff services complicate bureaucratic structure. Lack of tight coordination at the work level means that these functions are shoved farther up the management hierarchy, where they are attempted by managers with little or no technical knowledge of the project.

It is in this type of staff functions that professionalism still clashes with rigid bureaucratic procedures, and the remaining programming "craftsmen" occasionally brush up against the more even-tempered bureaucratic "gamesmen." Corporate systems of bureaucratic organization are at odds with those data-processing functions that are still performed in nonrationalized ways. Such conflicts diminish as an increasing number of data-processing tasks are made more routine.

Probably the biggest complaint heard from programmers and analysts is that corporate management does not understand them. Even humanistic, democratically oriented managers seemingly have but a temporary influence on the power of bureaucratic control. Often, attempts are made to inject job-enrichment, as if it were adrenalin, into tired projects. But these attempts are usually too little and often too late; and they do not attack the root of the problem, which is a definite conflict between cooperative work patterns and rigid formal hierarchy. Cooperative patterns are those that usually grow up naturally from the base of work in process. They reflect the ways workers choose to organize their activities so that they can get the work done and at the same time take pride in the way that they did it. Formal hierarchy is a vise that is fitted from the top down. Its function is to assure that the work is done. But it does more than that, for its strength seems to be that it is almost impervious to change from below.

The differences are in fact monumental. They are built on the foundation of totally different power relations. Co-operative work patterns usually reflect flexible and change-able power relations depending on the needs of the work and the workers. Hierarchy, on the other hand, and particularly its use along with systems of bureaucratic control, represents a rigid set of power relations. Although these are usually neutralized by terms such as authority and responsibility, there is little doubt about who has the power and who does not. Hierarchy acts as a social funnel, allowing directives to flow down and keeping change from forcing its way up. Bureaucratic control imbeds these relations into a set of rules and procedures. This further distorts our ability to see work structure as a social one rather than as a faceless organization.

CHAPTER

7

Technology

Management science attempts to provide a base from which corporate planners can *systematically* control and predict the actions of labor. Technology is developed within the same framework. Management policy defines the objectives and the actions of workers engaged in developing the technological products. Whereas the "hard" or physical sciences outline the limits of change, the social sciences, management included, detail the shape of change.

To be successful, computer technology has to meet the objectives of management science—by providing a more efficient way of doing something (faster and/or cheaper), and by doing it in a predictable way. To meet these objectives workers have to be subservient to the technology rather than the other way around. For those who argue that computer technology increased the overall skill level of workers, it is necessary to point out that such a phenomenon would be outside the objectives of management science and therefore outside the realm of design considerations. Computers were designed to minimize labor costs and to speed production. Skilled workers, even in small numbers, are expensive. Their ability to control knowledge also enables them to control their own actions, a situation that is quite unpredictable for management.

In general, technological change takes longer to develop and is more costly than other management design factors such as reorganization of the work process and modification in the organizational structure. Work method changes are relatively inexpensive compared to the lead time and cost involved in designing and installing new capital-intensive equipment or software.

In addition, technological design does not rest within the purview of the individual firm. A firm faced with declining labor productivity or unpredictable worker reactions will institute many other changes before seeking out new technological considerations. Firms using computers, for example, may have ideas about the way computer technology can be reorganized to better suit their needs, but they generally lack the development funds to bring about their own solutions. While Management science provides the ideology and methodology for changing technology, individual firms do not have as much flexibility in controlling this type of change. The needs of the firms using computers have interacted with the interests of the firms supplying the technology.

There is no single computer technology per se, but rather the development of many technologies. Some have been successful in that they met their design objectives; others have not. Technological history leaves us with a junkyard of ill-suited developments—developments that did not fit the demands of government and business users, and those that did not suit the interests of computer manufacturers, notably IBM.[1]

Computer technology has been molded by business and government demands as well as competitive pressure (and lack thereof) within the computer manufacturing sector. The literature of management science describes situations in which it may be necessary to trade efficiency in one part of an operation for increased efficiency in another. Computers present one such situation. The first organizations to introduce computers, banks and insurance companies, did so because their paper work was increasing rapidly, and with it their clerical labor costs. Some trade-off was required between a large number of clerical workers and the added expense of a few skilled technicians.[2] Early computers did require more skilled labor for their operation and programming, but it was hoped that this phenomenon would be transitory.

By the early sixties, second- and third-generation hardware and software design was addressed to this problem. Software improvements were aimed at increasing operator and programmer productivity. Hardware developments began to concentrate on the compatibility problem in order to reduce worker training costs and increase the interchangeability of data-processing workers. Developments in the 1970s have gone farther toward meeting management objectives without having to increase the skill level of *any* group of employees. Program packages and sophisticated software are aimed at eliminating the "middleman" from the computer hierarchy by letting workers outside the data-processing department use the computer system directly.[3]

The history of computer development outlines the movement from batch-processing systems toward continuous-flow technology. It is a movement that has occurred in other industries. In the production sector, industries such as oil and chemical, as well as auto and steel, have increasingly used continuous-flow technology. Computer development applied the same concepts to the flow of data within the service sector of the economy, and it did this at a time when the number of workers in the service sector was growing faster than the number in factory-related jobs.[4]

Until the third generation of computers, both computer hardware and software developments necessitated the processing of batches, or groups, of data. Batch-processing is not only slower than continuous, but it is also extremely dependent on the labor process. The early computer applications, for example, were made up of a large number of small steps, or procedures, each step dependent on the work done in the previous one. Usually the individual steps were linked by computer operators or clerks. In batch-processing systems the workers controlled the equipment, for they could control the pace of the process.[5]

Continuous-flow systems enable data to be processed the way oil is in a refinery—with little human intervention. Computer operators are removed from the flow of transactions because the operating system software now makes the routine decisions that used to define each step. Programmers are pushed farther into the background as decreasing hardware costs replace many programmer functions.

Computer technology has also progressed from a centralized system to that of a series of decentralized operations, thus matching the needs of business organizations. The reduction in equipment costs allows managers in all corporate departments to coordinate and control their data processing with the aid of minicomputers, which can be linked together with central management functions. Operational tasks can thus be carried out locally, and planning decisions can still be controlled by upper corporate management. This form of processing, called distributed data processing because it distributes computing power throughout the firm, is having a marked impact on data-processing workers. Routine programmer and operator functions that used to be performed in the centralized computer centers are now being done by clerical workers outside the data-processing department.

Distributed data processing—still quite new, with many problems yet to be worked out—was developed in reaction to the high cost of centralized data-processing installations in the 1960s. It is intended to allow corporate users to process their own information without intervention by operators and programmers. In addition, it meets the needs of corporate management strategy by facilitating the notion of matrix management, which allows managers to decentralize or pass down operational decisions within the hierarchy.[6]

Design objectives are framed by a combination of scientific possibility and society's priorities. In the case of computers, design objectives were also strongly influenced by government and military funding. Hardware developments owe their laboratory and initial application to military use. Developments such as vacuum tubes, transistors, lasers, and integrated circuits were all first tested on military projects. In the area of software, large-scale program development and timesharing capabilities were tried as early as the 1950s in the Semi-Automatic Ground Environment (SAGE) early-warning radar system. Not only was the software developed in this way, but procedures for training and dividing programming labor were also begun under the auspices of military projects.[7]

Federal funding, in general, was an important part of computer development. In 1968, for example, federal funds were used for half the research and development budgets of private industry. Not surprisingly, the "fastest growing sectors of the economy derive from science-based technological innovations that are strongly supported by the government."[8] Within the federal research and development budget, over 80 per cent of funds was sponsored by the Department of Defense and the space program administration.[9] Clearly, the needs of the military were being met in the *design* of computer technology.

While government funding played a big part in computer system design, IBM's marketing strategies have had a particularly important influence in shaping the *rate* of technology introduction. Although competition from other manufacturers helped reshape the design of some IBM systems, IBM's dominance has often forced would-be systems out of the marketplace.[10] As we have seen, General Electric's time-sharing innovations were years ahead of IBM's, yet IBM's control of the market finally led GE to scrap the project and then leave the computer business. GE testimony indicates that the company could not afford to take the multimillion dollar losses required to push its technology from development to mass use. Dr. Alan McAdams, an economist and chief government witness summarized the GE situation this way: "Capital, in private enterprise economy, is made available to those activities which are profitable. GE managers forecasted a seven-year breakeven period with losses of $700–$800 million, before it could be successful in the general purpose computer market."[11]

In a similar vein, RCA management made a conscious

decision *not* to invest in innovative design, but rather to focus research on copying and improving on IBM products. RCA plans called for developing machines that were hardware and software compatible with IBM in order to capture some of the IBM market, which was dependent on data-processing workers trained on IBM equipment. In developing the Series 70 computers, "RCA shifted their development people from new technology work to compatibility, thus disrupting their own design plans."[12] RCA's previous family of computers, the Spectra series, had offered "virtual memory" long before IBM even announced plans for it. Whatever new technology had been in the works was clearly closed off by RCA management's "compatibility strategy." McAdams argues that RCA did not control the "rate of technology innovations" because "IBM's market position endowed it with monopoly capital" that allowed the latter to cut off alternative developments. RCA, like GE, exited from the computer business in the early 1970s.

IBM's pricing strategies were a key to the company's ability to control the rate of technology introduction. The strategies allowed them not only to shape the technology, but also to shape corporate management objectives. According to Hilary Faw, the company's Director of Business Practices, IBM was able to create a new value system so that businesses would consider an IBM computer a necessity rather than a cost-justifiable investment. In a 1971 memo to Frank Cary, chairman of the board, he argued that:

> A new value (price) system had become established arbitrarily and artfully by IBM (the gross profits of that value system supported heavy investment in market growth and the 360 investment).

> During the early '60's, demand for data processing systems continued to outpace the supply. These systems, simple and limited as compared to today, came to be regarded as *necessities,* not capital asset acquisitions to be painstakingly evaluated for their potential return on investment.[13]

If computers could be portrayed as necessary status symbols, then managers would invest in them whether or not they proved successful in "displacing" costs. Their market price could therefore be determined by whatever methods IBM chose:

> By 1959, utilizing a "computer" had become a "prestige" factor in large and medium sized concerns, which caused a further depressing influence on displaceable cost as a criterion for placing an order. . . .
>
> The explosive growth of EDP after the 360 is a known fact. What is important to this discussion is that users ordered this equipment on a value system *related to the perceived and unquantified value of the predecessor systems.*[14]

Ironically, this "unquantifiable" value system, which proved successful in the 1960s, began to pose a problem for IBM in the 1970s: "Only in 1970, which marked the end of a decade of almost uninterrupted economic expansion, did users begin to question the issue of true economic value. The unbundling decision [government pressure that forced IBM to price separately each hard and software product] sharpened this questioning."[15]

In fact, the question was complicated by computer workers who, in Faw's terms, kept management from finding an answer to the value problem:

> The historical erosion of displaceable cost, combined with the existence of a *new breed of professional programmers interposed between top management and the in-house user* of the output, rendered all but impossible the gaining of any insight on what the value in fact was, or if indeed, any existed.
>
> Many additional factors of course contribute to the dilemma we and our users face as we begin to address quantification of value. The complexity of the machines and operating systems (which created

the requirement for professional systems programmers), management's inability and lack of motivation to understand the system; a delayed aware-
ness that hardware costs are moving down rapidly
while people costs are moving up sharply; *the
natural instinct for self-preservation among the
professionals, who are hence reluctant to have
management gain an understanding which could
result in reducing or eliminating the professional's
role,* etc.[16]

Data-processing workers have, of course, been blamed
with almost everything from "computer errors" to "elitism."
Faw's analysis of their role in IBM's pricing plans takes this
blame-the-victim syndrome one step farther. Their position
between management and technology gives them some
degree of control over their environment. As they are
removed from this position, and as their control diminishes,
they are obviously reluctant to give up their role. In fact,
their struggle to retain their knowledge and position gives
them the power to obscure management's understanding of
the technology and therefore its value. IBM policies have
been successful in controlling a number of variables that
presented barriers to the company's continued growth.
Control of labor, specifically data-processing labor, has
posed some major problems. Whether or not the company
can control these workers and their associated costs will, in
part, determine its corporate rate of growth and control
over the introduction of technology.

IBM's influence on the rate and type of available
technology has changed over time. Until the mid-seventies,
its strong monopoly position allowed the company to
establish prices beneficial to itself. As computer manufacturing costs declined, however, it became necessary for
IBM to price products in units that are both competitive and
more "rational" for computer users. The price of the
technology has of course had a marked impact on its
possible application. Cheaper "computing power" today
has expanded the use of computers to small businesses and

even individuals. The needs of these newer computer users will undoubtedly again reshape the design of the technology.

Technological innovation is nothing more or less than a process, which, like any other process, involves people from beginning to end. Technology-based products are shaped by the people who specify the design objectives *and* by the people who are affected by them. Technology's roots lie in the base of large-scale capital accumulation and its design reflects the objectives of that capital. Like the labor process, organization and development of technology must meet the goals of those who manage the capital. Far from being an independent force, successful technology is the result of many factors; factors that characterize the social organization and the market pressures of the capitalist society.

In meeting the needs of management, technological developments attempt to replace labor costs with machine costs. This process of labor "displacement" is intended to decrease the overall costs of the corporation as well as provide management with the tools that better control the worker and the work process. Until recently, computer technology was not necessarily successful in achieving overall cost reduction, but it seems to have been somewhat successful in tightening managerial control. Both the development of continuous-flow processing and the notion of distributed data processing have resulted in computer uses that more completely control the physical actions of workers. They are able to provide this control because the decision-making and thought-producing aspects of the work process have already been rationalized and incorporated into the technological design process. Faced with management control of the technological design process, it is not surprising that even computer workers feel locked-in by new computer systems. Their shopfloor actions, while more overtly influential in affecting management strategies for changes in labor process, worker behavior, and management organization, have a delayed and indirect affect on technology.

CHAPTER

8

Social Customs and Relations of the Workplace

Work organization, strongly influenced by management needs, is, of course, also shaped by worker background, interests, and needs. Data processing, like all other occupations, has a culture of its own, independent of management theory and practice. The culture, or social history, of a workplace reflects where workers come from, where they perceive that they are going, and the kind of environment they carve out to meet their needs. It portrays workers as people in pursuit of their own objectives, objectives that often clash with those of the organization. Because data processing is a comparatively new field, its social customs have not been deeply investigated. Gerald Weinberg on psychology and Philip Kraft on sociology do a wonderful job depicting the aspirations of programmers.[1] For the most part, however, the social history of data processing remains locked within work customs and jargon-filled shoptalk. We shall begin to pick out some of the customs that have helped shape the work process.[2]

Generally, the interests and problems of data-processing workers are like those found in the Department of Health, Education, and Welfare study *Work in America*.[3] Regardless of level within the data-processing hierarchy, the workers want personally satisfying work, which will give them a sense of accomplishment and can be done in pleasant social interaction with people whom they like. Like others weaned on the American Dream, they seek situations in which they can control their work environment in some way; maybe even be their own boss. Their problems stem from the contradictions between their seemingly sensible aspirations and the attainment of dreams within the routinized job structures they find. *Work in America* puts it succinctly:

> What the workers want most, as more than 100 studies in the past 20 years show, is to become masters of their immediate environments and to feel that their work and they themselves are important— the twin ingredients of self-esteem. Workers recognize that some of the dirty jobs can be transformed only into merely tolerable, but the most oppressive features of work are felt to be avoidable: constant supervision and coercion, lack of variety, monotony, meaningless tasks, and isolation. An increasing number of workers want more autonomy in tackling their tasks, greater opportunity for increasing their skills, rewards that are directly connected to the intrinsic aspects of work, and greater participation in the design of work and the formulation of their tasks.[4]

Even data-processing workers, with their image of glamor and in some cases professionalism, have been unable to control the circumstances that bridge the gap between aspirations and routine work. The social customs of the shopfloor, however, help them to create the environment that shuts out the more demeaning aspects of the work organization. Customs may not yet be strong enough to penetrate the walls of bureaucratic structure and rationalized work, but they do help to create a tolerable immediate environment. Job rationalization eats away at the very heart of work as it removes sources of self-satisfaction. Social customs provide a shell protecting the ego of the worker from the encroachment of fragmentation.[5]

Management theory and practice may wage fierce battles

over the heads of the workers, but as long as workers can control the actions on the shopfloor they feel that they are outside the range of battle. One data-processing worker summed it up this way: "I've been in this business for twenty years, and in many ways nothing has changed. Management has come along with lots of new bells and fancy whistles like structured coding and schedules, but we continue to do things the way we feel comfortable." In reality, the salvos of the war often land in their immediate area, causing data-processing jobs to become fragmented and subject to bureaucratic control. But as this process occurs the informal relations and culture of the work area help protect the worker from the onslaught of change. They also help to slow the pace and shape of management-induced change. Fragmented job structures produce fragmented social relations. In the midst of this process the sex, race, and class distinctions apparent in the larger society have been mirrored in the data-processing field. Although the novelty of the field did afford upward mobility to many groups during its heyday, this mobility has tended to stop at the boundaries of the fragmented job ladders.

The interests and aspirations of data-processing workers have changed very little over the last twenty years. What has changed is the jobs that they find themselves in. Despite the different ways that workers are selected and recruited, today's entrants seem to give priority to the same intrinsic values characteristic of the early data-processing generation. They still want jobs that offer challenge and self-satisfaction.

Creating a Social History

In the early days of data processing, workers were attracted by the status, pay, and upward mobility of its occupations. Today, the somewhat outdated image of these characteristics still continues to draw people. The field has been, and remains, a magnet pulling working-class youth with the lure of middle-class professionalism. Operations jobs, in particular, provided entry-level slots into the possibility of white-collar "clean" work:

> In New Orleans, at the Hibernia National Bank, David Burns is a 24-year-old computer operator who comes on like a banker—conservative dark suit, white shirt, neatly-trimmed hair with short sideburns. Four years ago he was working his way up the ladder in the Winn-Dixie Stores chain, taking junior college courses in business administration at night. A friend who worked for the bank suggested that he apply for a computer room job. . . . He likes his job, thinks it's a good job, and not really too difficult, although there's a lot to learn. He says his father is proud of his son's job as a computer operator, and Burns is proud of it himself.[6]

Entry through the ranks of programming has been possible for those whose families were comfortable enough to provide a college education. Though most programmers have come from middle-class homes, many are the first in their families to gain entry into the professional world:

> As a programmer I remember that the truly remarkable thing about the field was the fact that many of us were the first generation in our family to go to college. In the shops that I worked in during the fifties and sixties, there were a lot of Jews, Italian and Polish men and women. It was a big deal for our families and, of course, really important to us. How else could a Jew get entry into the corporate world?

In the early sixties, this upward mobility was even extended to women. At a time when few occupations were open to them, programming was comparatively an open door: "When I graduated from college in 1963 I walked the pavements for six months—nobody would hire a woman except to type. I found out about programming, took the test, and bingo, there I was—a professional, and a woman no less."

Given the status of the field, and the comparative ease of

entry, it is not surprising that workers have had high job expectations. A 1963 study found that programmers focused on the intrinsic values of the job. Characteristically, they were looking for nonroutine, creative work that would offer them intellectual challenge in their search for satisfaction.[7] Although no similar study has been done for operators, I have found that, in general, they tend to look for the same satisfactions, with less weight on intellectual challenge.

Because operations positions require less formal education they often attract workers whose experiences and family background have deemphasized education. Like many working-class youth, they experienced intimidation by the school system, which left them uninterested in further intellectual "challenge": "I never did well in school. I hated it. All I want to do is get enough training so that I can get a good job where I can have responsibilities and feel important. I don't want a job where I have to think a lot, that would remind me of school." Operators experience challenge from the desire to exercise responsibility. In the machine room, operators see themselves pitted against the machine, where even in rationalized situations they match their wits against the chaos of pressure. The need for challenge remains; its definition has changed.[8]

Today, although more jobs fall within routine structures, new workers still have the same interests and objectives as those a generation ago. Even the selection process that seeks conforming personalities does not screen out the intensity of their aspirations. Workers preparing for operations and coding jobs at lower levels continue to set their sights on self-actualizing goals. Of course they want money, and they want to get ahead, but they also hope and plan for jobs whose work will make them feel useful and important, work that gives them some pride in a job well done.

In the community college where I teach most of the students come from inner-city, underprepared educational backgrounds, yet their interests point to intrinsic values traditionally attainable only in the most professional jobs. As part of their preparatory job training, students are given a questionnaire in which they are asked to rank the job characteristics they expect to find satisfying when they begin work. We find that students rank "to be independent," "to do interesting work," and "to do different things" at the top of their lists.[9]

Social scientists often argued that high job aspirations are created by increased education. They would have us believe that people expect inner rewards from work because they have been educated to want them. But this confuses length of education with personal goals. People do stay in school longer today than they did a generation ago, but as *Work in America*, puts it, "The demand for higher academic credentials has not increased the prestige, status, pay or difficulty of the job."[10] According to Ivar Berg, the majority of Americans are overeducated for the jobs that they hold.[11] That computer operators may be more likely to have a community college education today does not make them any more likely to want personal satisfaction from work. They always wanted self-esteem, and regardless of how routine their jobs may become, they continue wanting it. I found that students returning from the most routine data-processing jobs ranked factors for job satisfaction as they had done before entering the job market. One student, after several years in a clerical input/output control job, said: "I could do the job in my sleep now. There's just no challenge, so I'm looking around for another job. I'd say my interests are the same as they were when I graduated; I want to do something worthwhile and get to do different things."

The environment data-processing workers find is socially and architecturally stratified along the lines of most corporate work. In an urban setting the stratification is bound to be played out vertically, with the most routine work being performed on the lowest floors and the higher level staff functions housed "upstairs." This architectural hierarchy is so common that it has become a part of most workers' vocabulary. Programmers, for example, might say "the guys upstairs want us to come in on time" or "send the keypunching down to the machine floor." Data entry and clerical input/output functions are found, along with the machine room, on the lower floors (sometimes even in the basement), whereas programming and systems analysis get the more scenic views. A programmer in New York was surprised to find that the large company for which she worked was no different from others:

> In our shop there were two machine rooms; the more routine business functions were on a lower floor than the bigger new computer. The place was so structured that the pool of applications programmers sat on a lower floor than systems programmers. Of course, staff consultants were up there with the big brass on the higher floors. At first I didn't think anything of it, I thought that it was unique to our company and the data-processing work, but then I found out that the places where my friends worked all looked the same.

Suburban companies stretch their stratification horizontally. Factors such as parking spaces and proximity to a window become the symbols of higher position.

Social stratification is built into the hierarchy with almost as much permanence as the architectural divisions. According to a 1974 study only 13 per cent of the business systems analysts are likely to be women, and 20 per cent of business programmers may be women. At the other end of the hierarchy, 99 per cent of keypunch or data-entry operators are women, with 20 per cent of machine-room operations positions going to women.[12] Statistics for discrimination of minority ethnic and racial groups are not generally available, although my experience and interviews found strong evidence of this type of stratification. I found, not surprisingly, that operations and lower-level coding jobs are filled by members of minority groups, and in the higher levels in the data-processing hierarchy fewer minorities appear. In part this reflects differences in educational entry requirements, but it also reveals some characteristics of discrimination within corporate structure.

Corporate policy establishes the general rules, descriptions, and requirements for all positions within the corporation—allowing upper management to open or close the gates for affirmative action programs. Data-processing jobs, like all others, are set under such policies. In *Industry and Labor*, Andrew Friedman reminds us that "top managers *do not create racism and sexism*, but they do use these divisions among workers to their advantage."[13]

Social stratification is also controlled from within the department. In data processing two factors reinforce corporate policies of separation. The first is the tendency for people in a group to work closely with one another and identify with the peers in their group. Peer identification is obviously exclusionary. Although the motives of each member may be remarkably free from discrimination, the end result is the same. Workers and their immediate supervisors tend to pull together and "keep to their own kind." Because first-line managers and, in many cases, supervisors are in a position to hire or promote, this type of discrimination is rampant. Like the operations supervisors who say they would hire a woman except that she "wouldn't fit in," the characteristics of each group hold the line against intrusion from outside. Lower level workers particularly have grown up in an environment in which they see one working-class group fighting off encroachment from another. It is not unusual to see operations shops where most workers are black, or Puerto Rican, or Italian, or whatever concentration of working-class people live in the surrounding area. When an important intrinsic value of the job concerns the social relations of the workplace, it is no wonder that workers will try to hire their "own kind."

Another form of social demarcation appears at higher levels within the department, where the internalization of corporate goals begins to take on more importance. Workers are expected to act in accordance with the behavioral traits of bureaucratic structure. Failure to exhibit the correct traits stands in the way of promotion. Discrimination is enforced by trait-rating. A woman who rose to a high programming staff position described her climb:

One paid a price for mobility. At first I was pleased that as a woman from a Polish family, I had become so successful. After a while I realized that I had become two people; one, on the job, was no longer Polish—I had to dress, act, and speak like everyone else. When I went home at the end of the day I was really schizophrenic.

Trait-rating is done with the sanitized jargon of management theory.[14] As we have seen, it is implemented by performance-evaluation sessions in which managers grade workers on a series of criteria. Its message is clear to minority groups struggling to gain entry into higher levels: adopt the dominant group's behavioral characteristics or stay where you are. For many the choice is an unconscious one. Although they may *think* they want to progress up the ladder, the adoption of ruling ideological traits is so uncomfortable they stay where they are: ·"When I first started it looked like my family could say 'Look, Italian boy makes good in data processing.' But now it seems that I can only go so far. I'm not even sure that I would want to go farther up in management; people are so different up there."

For many, it becomes clear that whatever upward mobility exists tends to stop at the limits established by the job ladders.[15] Many companies hire operators with the promise that they can go into programming after "a while," but most of the operators I spoke to seemed to think that this was more of a promise than a reality. One frustrated operator explained:

It's really "Catch 22." You have to do well in operations for them to consider you for programming, but if you do well they don't want to let you go because they're afraid they won't be able to get another good operator. It happens occasionally, but it's so rare it's more like window dressing. I ask them every few months if it's time for me to go into programming, but they always have some excuse.

Applications programmers meet the same roadblocks when they look for transfers to systems programming, and some programming ranks are totally divorced from analysis ladders, making it difficult for workers in them to change paths.

On the shopfloor, architectural and social distinctions collapse to form limiting physical mobility patterns. Operators are stuck in the machine room, which in an increasing number of companies is electronically controlled by identification passes.[16] Although entrance to the machine room confers status, which even most programmers no longer have, operators nevertheless cannot roam from their station. Machine rooms, air-conditioned for the sake of the equipment, are incredibly noisy. Normal conversational tone is impossible and, particularly in the area of the printers, operators have to shout to make themselves heard over the roar of the equipment.

Programmers' status is usually reflected by the height of their cubicle walls. In most companies, programmers and junior-level analysts are kept in "areas" or "pools," which are cordoned off by file cabinets or three-quarter-high partitions. Higher level analysts and project leaders may be given offices with walls to the ceiling if their jobs require interaction with people outside the data-processing department.[17] Generally, programmers have the freedom to wander from their cubicles and around the "area," but their mobility is usually restricted to programming territory. Unless they are given permission to speak to a data-processing user they are expected to stay in their area.

As one might expect, the noise level can be quite high, and programmers learn to "tune out" conversations that surround them. In addition, as terminals increasingly become part of the programmers' immediate workplace, the noise level from these devices grows steadily worse.[18] Initially, a terminal in one's cubicle was a status symbol, but now, between the increased noise level and the increased flow of traffic as programmers "drop in" to use it, a terminal is usually a hindrance.

A recent study by a software firm found that programmer

productivity could be increased as much as 41 per cent by installation of terminals in and near programmer cubicles. The survey showed that the increase was a result of the 80 per cent reduction in walking time. They found that "typically [a programmer] makes eight to ten trips away from his desk each day," and their logic asserts that terminals make walking unnecessary and therefore help increase programmer "productive" time.[19] Programmers, on the other hand, insist that their walking time *is* productive because they are thinking. Even first-line managers tend to agree: "When you're coding all day, you have to get up and walk around—stretch your mind and your body." But as the movement toward coding at terminals continues, the physical mobility of programmers decreases.

In general, data-processing workers have three major complaints about their work: poor management; lack of challenge and diversity; and limitations on seeing the "big picture." These complaints are not new. A 1963 study found that management's lack of understanding and appreciation led the list of programmers' reasons for leaving a job, followed by their dissatisfaction with the monotonous nature of the work.[20] As programming has been deskilled and rationalized, these complaints have increased. One observer commented on the effects this had on the individual: "In programming, the use of assembly-line organization can destroy the intellectual work satisfactions which motivate programmers, and the contradiction between the monotony of work and the difficulty can bring about neurosis."[21]

My experiences reiterate these findings for both programmers and operators. As in other occupations, their on-the-job experience gives them a strong sense of what is wrong and what could be done in a better way.[22] The more bureaucratic the corporate structure the more intense the rumblings of discontent. But even in the more "people-oriented" firms, I found that programmers and operators had well-developed opinions on other ways of doing things.

Much of the expression of these complaints is limited to

gripe sessions, which do not immediately threaten management control; they have learned not to push their discontent beyond their supervisors. Workers are given the message that "gripe sessions are O.K., but you don't know enough about management to change things," thus spreading the cloak of managerial mystification over most management directives. Workers may tell each other that this is "bullshit," but the indoctrination is so complete that most are afraid of testing their ideas. Those who do are often branded "troublemakers," a mark that clearly shortens their job tenure. *Managerial mystification is a particularly brutal exercise of raw power.* As Richard Sennet and Jonathan Cobb point out, "A sense of self-doubt intervenes to make workers unsure they *have the right* to fight back."[23]

If workers do not directly confront management with their ideas, they are rarely at a loss to describe their thoughts to coworkers. An operator described the feelings of many:

> If you really want to know what I would do differently I'll tell you. First thing, I'd give the operators better training, then I'd let them run more of their own show. Sure, sure, we have to keep logs of what comes in and goes out, but numbers aren't everything. I could keep this shop on schedule, and fill out all their stupid records if they would only let me do it. Me and a couple of good guys who were trained to know what we were doing, and who really cared—we could get it all done right.

Programmers, analysts, and even project leaders spell out the same kind of dreams. If only they had some degree of control over what they were doing. If only they had better knowledge. Although these are people whose job titles allow them to retain more "professional expertise" than operators, their frustrations are strikingly similar, as in this case of a program analyst:

> You know that with all the things like on-line debugging, structured code, pre-compilers, and constant machine turn-around, programmer pro-

ductivity has not increased. To me it's simple: the more they give us smaller and smaller pieces of the total pie, the more we feel insignificant in the corporate structure. With jobs structured this way, why should we care.

If I were to do anything about it, I would start by giving people more responsibility, instead of less. Of course, you'd have to give them something worthwhile to work on and the chance to make decisions which affect their work. Then you'd see some programmer productivity!

Creating a Workable Environment

Gripe sessions may be the most common overt form of expression, but workers also act indirectly to control their environment. In the activity that takes almost half of each waking day they manage skillfully to inject activities that make work more interesting. Short of restructuring the "system," workers do influence those things that affect their daily lives. In many cases their actions have repercussions up and down the "system."

One of the most common forms of worker activity is the creation of social networks to displace the weight of official bureaucratic organization. For the overwhelming majority of data-processing workers with whom I have come in contact, "other people" is the chief reason for staying on a job (except money, of course). I have seen workers stay on a job in the midst of generally acknowledged intolerable conditions, because "the people in the shop are so great, I really like being with them." Not only does this spirit provide the base for informal work groups, it also spills over into luncheons for special occasions, evening drinking rounds, and, of course, parties. One woman described her shop in the 1960s as one where "everyone was married to, engaged to, or dating someone else in the department."

On the job, the socializing turns into game-playing as a way of "letting off steam." Every occupation has an outlet for pressure, and data processing is no exception. Workers are often told that their pranks are "behavior unworthy of a professional," but neither moral persuasion nor outright authority seems to put a halt to game-playing. To make the shift go faster, operators sometimes tap out rhythms on the equipment or have mock races to time their "expertise" at tape mounting or responding to operating system commands. In the "old" days when operators had more contact with people outside the machine room, they ran betting pools on everything from sports to the number of programmer errors. Now, with the increase in isolated machine centers, operators continue their activities with the aid of computer terminals. Given the chance, they will transmit personal messages to terminals in use by their friends or send messages back to programmers. Many small computer centers are linked to larger ones through these communications networks. An operator in a small center explained how important the network was to her: "It's really exciting, because my shop is so small I hardly get to meet anybody. I've gotten a blind date through the network and also picked up some friends. I bet a quarter of the messages floating through the system are not from the Operating System, but from people trying to talk to each other."

Of course programmers also play games.[24] In addition to the traditional word games such as crossword puzzles and "Hangman," they too use their terminals for communicating with one another. Messages range from "Joe, call your wife" to "Help, I'm stuck in a programming loop." Terminals also provide a source of prepackaged game-playing. Many on-line systems have games like "football," chess, and "Star-trek," which are rapidly catching on as intercomputer-center pastimes. Inventing and coding new games is a favorite of many programmers: "I stayed up all night once trying to write the code for a program that would play that new game called 'Mastermind.' Hell, you'd never find me spending that much time on one of 'their' problems." When pushed into coding for long periods at a time, programmers have been known to insert messages that are sometimes unflattering to management in the midst of their programs. In shops where coding is not controlled by rationalized procedures (that is, structured code), many programmers will name sections of their code after family members or private jokes.

For the most part, game-playing is a harmless way of getting breathing space in an otherwise pressurized day. Middle-level and "upstairs" managers may complain that the workers do not look productive, but most activities are tolerated as long as they do not "interfere with the work that has to be done." Periodically, most shops have a crackdown, when upper management warns and threatens against "unproductive" behavior. But usually these are short-lived and shop culture regains its foothold.

From the perspective of management, only a thin line divides shopfloor pranks from tactics aimed at management. Workers distinguish between computer crime (an individual stealing funds from a computer system) and computer sabotage (willfully aimed at the company); management policy is terrified of both. To managers who feel under seige, those "harmless" messages floating through the system represent secret plans that might lead to taking over the computer center. The U.S. Chamber of Commerce estimated that in 1976 computer crime may have cost business $100 million. Companies are reluctant to talk about it for fear that they might damage their image with their customers.[25] The first computer crime bill has just been introduced in the Senate with stiff penalties. Senator Ribicoff, the bill's sponsor, hopes that these penalties, "unprecedented in federal criminal law for white-collar crime, will deter the potential computer thief and, at the same time, pose a warning to all white-collar criminals that Congress sees white-collar crime as a threat to our society which should be dealt with in a manner befitting a crime."[26]

Yet disgruntled programmers and operators do look for revenge for frustration, and to the extent that they retain some technical knowledge it is possible for them to vent their anger. Generally, these are individualist rather than collective responses. To many observers it is amazing that "rip-off" or sabotage does not occur more often: "As a systems analyst I have a bit of felon in me. Well, you know, we spend so much time defining and solving problems I wouldn't be surprised if most programmers and analysts weren't 'closet felons.' There is so much temptation, and yet it practically never happens." Because the possibility of computer crime is so strong, management endlessly addresses itself to methods of preventing it.[27] Workers who are fired, for whatever reason, are usually given enough time only to clear their desks, and sometimes not even that. Elaborate systems of manual and electronic controls are built into most accounting programs. And over the past ten years, the role of data-processing auditor has grown in importance as an increasing number of companies try weeding out program bugs and operator procedures that might cause financial concern to the company. But most shopfloor managers freely admit that still plenty of room exists for crime and sabotage. If anything, the lack of it is confusing to management. Most computer crime, at least that which makes its way into trade journals and newspapers, concerns individuals stealing from the system rather than a general expression of worker frustration.

It is more common for data-processing workers to give vent to their frustrations by slowing down, "working to rule," and attempting to control at least those small decisions that effect an impact on the pace of work.[28] Programmers, for example, almost always "fudge" their time estimates for completing a program or project. Whenever possible they will give themselves some breathing space by claiming complexity in the program. When all else fails, programs and essential documentation somehow manage to get lost.[29] Operators use the same tactics and augment them with "hardware malfunction" when other measures do not succeed. In short, data-processing workers apply the same practices of social custom as do workers in other jobs in order to structure their day and escape from constant pressure. Usually, these informal responses are made with unspoken cooperative effort.

Socializing, games, and slow-downs are informal methods of "testing the water" to see what can be done without bringing down the wrath of management. Workers check one another out and discover in a relaxed, nonthreatening way what activities are tolerated. The relations built through these social activities can bud into work organization and some degree of work control. Because collective activities and relations with people are so important on the shopfloor, it is not surprising that more energy is exerted in this more positive way than in individualistic acts of anger.

Most shops have their legendary "crack" groups; those programmers and operators who can get anything done. Whenever I asked what made such a group successful, people would tell me that "they did things their own way." A programmer, for example, related her experience in developing a fairly large-scale system:

> Everyone told us that collective decision-making just wouldn't work. But we did it. We designed and built a system from beginning to end, and we did it by jointly sharing the work and planning our efforts. I guess you could say that we worked by consensus. We had people at different levels working in the group, but anyone who felt that they needed to would call a meeting and we would all get together to decide how to solve a problem. I think the product we produced was really excellent, and management was also pretty pleased.

In another case, Gerald Weinberg describes a programming team working so tightly together that management decided to break up the group when it was clear that the managers no longer had control over the individuals in the group:

> The achievement of this group was so evident that the management of the company decided to give them a cash award. In typical management fashion, they gave the award to the person who had been designated as the group's manager. Imagine their bewilderment when he told them that he could not accept the award unless it was given to all.[30]

Management attempts to split the group were thwarted by the entire group leaving for another company.

Operators who perform remarkable feats in the machine room are few and far between from management's standpoint, but every worker knows who they are. A shift supervisor discussed what made these workers different: "Well, for one thing, they'll look for a problem to solve, and use the machine to try things out whenever there is a slow period. For another, they usually help and cover for each other so they can get more time to experiment. It's unusual to find just one 'super' operator, usually they motivate each other." These "super teams" seem to spring up like weeds in sidewalk cracks, whenever the opportunity arises. Their development is dependent on lower managers who, if they do not give grudging support, at least look the other way. In fully rationalized shops, where the actions of workers are proscribed by detailed rules, these "crack" groups are part of history. Yet their feats remain part of the shoptalk. Old-timers, who in data-processing terms are workers with "a few years under their belts," pass the stories on to new trainees. The characteristics of almost all the stories are remarkably similar: they tell of workers who respect one another, take pride in their work, and produce results that reinforce pride in themselves.

From a management perspective, super groups and collective work pose some difficult contradictions. On the one hand, these groups usually produce excellent results, but on the other, their cooperative responses are hard to combat. They highlight the conflict between what managers call efficient work and effective results.[31] Work organization controlled by the workers is most often *effective* in that it is done carefully and thoughtfully, but in terms of the total organization it may not be *efficient* because it cannot be controlled or predicted by management.

Combating cooperative responses leads to more control measures, which in turn lead to new forms of worker resistance. Managers who thought that they had solved the "programmer productivity problem" by placing terminals in the cubicles only find that they now do not know how to deal with the strange messages floating through the system. Locking operators in the machine room only increases their likelihood of "acting stupid because they can't find the answer to a problem." Because data-processing workers exhibit such strong occupational and peer loyalties, management has trouble making them focus on corporate goals. The ability to focus on corporate objectives is a key link in management theory. Most theory starts from the assumption that the goals of the individual and those of the enterprise are in tandem or can be brought together. As corporate loyalty breaks down in the face of occupational interest groups, the chain of management command loses an important link.

The social customs and relations of the shopfloor contradict those imposed by management objectives, which are aimed at controlling the actions and beliefs of workers. They represent a set of power relations that attempt to mold the consciousness of workers by formally imbedding control in the management superstructure. Shopfloor culture helps return self-respect to the individual by reinforcing the individual's right and ability to make decisions as well as the right to enjoy one's work. Although they do not have the power of management-imposed relations, workplace customs do show that there are other ways to do things—methods that do not necessarily alienate the individual. Significantly, the informal relations of the shopfloor illustrate that workers can and do take interest in and responsibility for work.

alization, and new technological developments would increase their productivity, as well as upgrade their profession. Accepting these arguments to some extent, workers were always struck by apparent contradictions on the shopfloor. Changes that were to increase their productivity and skills instead made them uninterested and less knowledgeable about their work, often less motivated and less productive. For the most part, they reacted against these so-called efficiency changes.

Changes in the nature of data-processing jobs followed the general principles established by management science. The work process was divided and specialized in order to isolate individual tasks that could be given to separate workers. Conceptual tasks such as systems analysis were separated from more routine chores such as programming, and the most repetitive functions were assigned to operations positions. Furthermore, the tools used by each group were simplified so that each step in the work process could become more repetitive. Operating systems, for example, were developed to simplify the work process of both operators and programmers. As these systems became more sophisticated, they assumed worker functions, incorporating directly into the computer hardware and software decision-making that formerly had been done by people.

Yet managers complained that divided labor created additional problems. In many situations, work processes that had been divided could not be put back together again. Since operators no longer knew the functions of the operating system, they were not able to handle nonroutine production problems. Similarly, programmers who were trained in only one application had no comprehensive view.

Management procedures also brought about a change in worker behavior on the job. Selection, educational, and motivational strategies were employed to make data-processing workers better fit the corporate mold. Somewhat successful in weeding out the programmers who, in the early days, had caused culture shock within the corporate walls, they did not seem to increase worker motivation or productivity. In fact, although increased quantitative efficiency was demanded, managers were also looking for greater control over the workers themselves.

In addition, the organization of management functions was modified to give management more control over actions on the shopfloor. Rigid forms of hierarchy and bureaucratic structure were superimposed on the data-processing workplace. As decision-making rules were codified, procedures for making decisions were pushed farther up the management hierarchy and away from shopfloor actions. Behind the seemingly rational facade of depersonalized rules lay a set of power relations that vested authority in the organizational structure. Thus, workers could no longer blame the boss; instead, they had to face an impersonal system. Management claimed that these forms of organization were made necessary by the size and complexity of corporate functions. When we look down to the bottom of the organizational hierarchy, however, we find that workers, whenever possible, work cooperatively and without the shackles of bureaucratic procedures.

Technology too was redesigned to fit the changing work process better. Both the hardware and software of computer technology were developed to allow for more continuous processing with less human intervention. As the manu-facturing costs of computer hardware decrease, it becomes possible for management to replace more human labor with comparatively inexpensive, consistent equipment. This type of technological change did not fall from the sky. It was not the result of independent inventors accidentally creating new computer technology. In fact, computer systems changed because they were designed to do so, and the design of these changes fit within the objectives of management science.

Management maintains that the tools of its trade are necessary for efficiency of the resource it calls labor. They always fall back on the position that division of labor and job rationalization are required for increased productivity. Yet one of the biggest issues in the trade literature is the growing "people cost." Although the quoted numbers do vary, management accepts figures that show data-processing labor costs gaining an increasing share of total data-processing costs, and computer hardware expenses declining. Dr. Richard Tanaka, then President of the International Federation of Information Processing, warned, for example, that by 1985, 90 per cent of data-processing costs will be attributable to labor.[1] It is now estimated that labor costs make up 75 per cent of the corporate data-processing budget.[2] If management has not been able to increase worker output significantly, it has been able to increase the predictability of workers and maintain a status quo for social as well as economic values, indicating the importance of social control as an objective of management strategy.

But the social-control aspects of efficiency do take their toll on the accumulation process within capitalism. I have seen a remarkable number of situations in which management controls *conflict* with worker productivity—situations in which workers cannot produce more because either their knowledge or motivation or both have been taken away. Restricting the movements of programmers and operators, for example, may give the illusion of increasing productivity, but it mainly serves to tighten control over their actions. To both programmers and operators, mobility means the opportunity to talk with others, a chance to "blow off steam," and often a chance to learn about what goes on in the total data-processing picture. Everyone on the shopfloor knows that operators are usually better operators if they get the chance to see and understand how their actions mesh with the rest of the structure. Similarly, programmers who are involved in more diversified tasks, and who have the freedom to talk with other workers, are considered "well-rounded" and therefore better workers. But management policy trades this form of worker productivity for their own version, which stamps greater control.

The differences between the ways that workers organize their activities and the ways that managers organize them are quite major, greater than what management simply calls the "labor-management problem." Management theory recognizes that the interests of labor and of capital may not always mesh, but it seeks to minimize the difference through "good" management policy. But I suggest that "good" management policy, whether it follows the outlines of theory X or theory Y, is but another patch in the worn-out quilt of divided jobs, controlled workers, and bureaucratic structure.

What is done in the name of efficiency for capitalism can be crippling for the functioning of the individual. Work that subdivides thoughts and actions can, as Marx put it, "attack the individual at the very roots of his life."[3] These mechanisms of efficiency are not at all natural; they are a method of social control.

We know from shopfloor discussions in data processing as well as in other fields that the present organization of work is decidedly inefficient in human terms. Workers complain of boredom, lack of interest, and the loss of self-esteem. They argue that if they were allowed to do the job the way they think it should be done, they would feel better about themselves and about the results of their labor. Management theory acknowledges these complaints with plans for job-enrichment and increased worker participation, but such schemes do not change the social relations of the workplace—they only help management better control human behavior.

Social relations are the way people interact. The social relations of the workplace are shaped by rigid hierarchies, bureaucratic procedures and divided tasks. This type of social arrangement concentrates power at the top. The social relations created by management science are not neutral, for they enforce the objectives of the economic system. If the organization of work is to change, both the economic objectives *and the social relations* have to change.[4]

The present organization of work reflects the political and other power relations within the larger society. Although these power relations are hidden behind what seem to be impartial rules and procedures, they sharply delimit the consciousness of workers, by attempting to strip them of the power to control their own activities. But there are, in fact, two sets of social relations—one created and enforced by management policy and another that grows out of the activities on the shopfloor. In order to have better control over human behavior, management theory, from Taylor's Scientific Management to the current management science, has attempted to remove knowledge from workers' control and put it within the sphere of management.

Knowledge and ideas are historically dangerous weapons. Management strategy may not always succeed in increasing productivity, but it attempts at least to keep knowledge and ideas in check. Management tools for controlling jobs, workers, and organization seek to remove knowledge as a potential weapon. But although concrete job knowledge may be taken away, ideas still remain—ideas that influence the shop culture, and that can continue to impact the organization of work. It is interesting that after twenty years of structured change, data-processing workers enter the field with the same dreams and goals. It is even more interesting that, on the job, the images of their goals and the ideas for attaining them do not fade.

Data-processing workers have developed workplace activities and cooperative work practices that stand in sharp contrast to the rationalized bureaucratic hierarchy imposed by management. We are told that human nature is competitive and individualistic, but data-processing shopfloor actions contradict this. Effective data-processing work is usually accomplished by workers who help one another by sharing knowledge, skills, and tasks. By sharing knowledge data-processing workers have created, in effect, their own shopfloor culture that gives workers at least the ability to tolerate the contradictions they face every day on the job. In addition, it can also become the basis from which data-processing workers can resist the further degradation of their jobs. The shopfloor struggle, which management calls the "labor-management problem," is really a struggle for dignity and economic survival. The nature of this struggle will continue to transform the character of data-processing work, just as it has done in the past.

When I began this study I examined management

justifications for efficiency and tried to compare these to what was actually taking place in the work environment. The more I looked the greater I found the differences between management and worker strategies for workplace activity. The contradictions between these two organizational forms suggest some interesting areas for further study. If we explore the cooperative and collective work groups that arise in the midst of bureaucratic structures we get a better idea of the nonfragmented methods people use when reorganizing work. If we look at the ways people try to learn more and often upgrade and enhance their jobs we see that self-respect and "doing a good job" play an important part in shopfloor activity. The way that work is now divided and organized by management is not fixed, nor is it inevitable. Work does *not* have to be organized to control human behavior. Efficient work activities can take place without the management ideology of social control. Examining workplace activities begins to point us in the direction of understanding other forms of work organization.

Notes,
Bibliography,
and
Index

Notes

Chapter 1

1. A. P. Ershov, "Aesthetics and the Human Factor in Programming," *Communications of the ACM* 15 (July, 1972), p. 503.

2. See Gary S. Becker, *Human Capital; A Theoretical and Empirical Analysis, with Special Reference to Education,* 2d ed. (New York: National Bureau of Economic Research, Columbia University Press, 1975). Those who follow the "human capital" argument see education as an investment that people might make to improve their productivity in the labor market. Like other investments, expenditure for education involves sacrificing current income in order to accrue benefits in the future.

3. Ivar Berg, with Sherry Gorelick, *Education and Jobs: The Great Training Robbery* (New York: Frederick A. Praeger, 1970).

4. U.S. Department of Health, Education and Welfare, *Work in America* (Cambridge: MIT Press, 1973), p. xvi.

5. Charles Lecht, *Waves of Change* (New York: Advanced Computer Techniques, 1977), p. 8.

6. Harry Braverman, *Labor and Monopoly Capital, The Degradation of Work in the Twentieth Century* (New York: Monthly Review Press, 1974), Chap. 4.

7. Ibid., p. 211

8. Karl Marx, *A Contribution to the Critique of Political Economy* (New York: International Publishers, 1972), p. 21.

9. Richard Sennett and Jonathan Cobb, *The Hidden Injuries of Class* (New York: Vintage Books, 1972), p. 208.

10. A major portion of the material in Part II is drawn from my experiences in the field and the detailed interviews conducted for this

study. Using a question guide that I developed in several preliminary test interviews, I conducted a dozen in-depth interviews (three to five hours) with people who had been in the field at least ten years, and twenty shorter discussions (approximately one hour each) with newer data-processing workers. Some of the longer sessions were taped, but I found that I was more comfortable taking extensive notes during the interviews.

11. Data-processing trade journals are full of articles about the problems of managing programmers. The study of programming and programmers has been included in the social sciences; psychologists and sociologists have begun examining changes in this occupation (see Part II). Yet comparatively little interest has been shown in the area of computer operations. It is not clear if this is because operations jobs have already undergone more change and now present fewer problems for management, or because the lack of data has blocked further study. Whatever the reason, I hope that the information presented here prompts further study of this group of workers.

Chapter 2

1. Parts of this chapter are based on an earlier article. See Joan Greenbaum, "Division of Labor in the Computer Field," *Monthly Review* 28, no. 3, (July-August 1976), pp. 40–55; also in *Technology, the Labor Process, and the Working Class* (New York: Monthly Review Press, 1976).

2. Gerald W. Brock, *The U.S. Computer Industry, A Study of Market Power* (Cambridge, Mass.: Ballinger Publishing Co., 1975), p. 12.

3. See, for example, Robert J. Canning and Roger L. Sisson, *The Management of Data Processing* (New York: John Wiley and Sons, 1967). This is an important point, brought out in most data-processing management books. Managers are warned not to attempt the computer processing of any application that is not already well defined. See also U.S. Department of Labor, Bureau of Labor Statistics, *Studies of Automatic Technology, No. 2,* "The Introduction of an Electronic Computer in A Large Insurance Company (October 1955). This case study traces the factors that influenced an insurance company to automate a record-keeping function.

4. U.S. Department of Commerce, Bureau of the Census, *U.S. Statistical Abstracts,* "Flow of Funds Accounts," annual.

5. *Life Insurance Fact Book* (New York: Institute of Life Insurance), annual.

6. Alan F. Westin and Michael Baker, *Databanks in A Free Society* (New York: Quadrangle Books, 1972), p. 222. For statistics on transaction increases during this period, see charts, pp. 224–27.

7. Memo from Hilary Faw, IBM Director of Business Practices, to Frank Cary, Chairman of the Board, Dec. 10, 1971; entered in evidence at *U.S. vs. IBM*, anti-trust trial, 1977.

8. "A Profile of the Programmer," a study by Deutsch and Shea, Inc. (New York: Industrial Relations News, 1963), pp. 8–31.

9. "Survey and Study of the Computer Field," *Computers and Automation,* January 1963, p. 23.

10. Dick Brandon and Fredrick Kirch, "The Case for D. P. Standards," *Computers and Automation,* November 1963, pp. 28–31.

11. Ibid.

12. Ibid., p. 29.

13. See Charles Lecht, *Waves of Change* (New York: Advanced Computer Techniques, 1977), Chap. 1.

14. Philip Kraft, *Programmers and Managers* (New York: Springer-Verlag, 1977), p. 97.

15. Definitions of the tasks performed by computer programmer and operator jobs have changed over time, although there are some common characteristics that have remained the same. The characteristics of tasks listed below—generally performed by people in these occupational titles—are compiled from U.S. Department of Labor, Bureau of Labor Statistics reports, notably the *Occupational Outlook Handbook,* which is issued every two years: *Computer programmers:* convert business, scientific, or engineering problems into a coded form that can be understood by computer. Depending on the level of experience, they may analyze a problem, determine the necessary steps to solve it, flowchart the logic of a solution, and code and test the procedures. *Computer operators:* monitor and operate the equipment used in a computer processing system. The equipment consists of a main console (control panel) and various input/output devices.

16. Kraft, pp. 93–95.

17. *Computerworld,* December 12, 1976, p. 12.

18. U.S. Dept. of Labor, Bureau of Labor Statistics, *Computer Manpower Outlook*, Bulletin 1826, 1974, p. 12.

19. "The 1970's: Retrospect and a Look Ahead," *Business Automation* (January 1972).

20. Ibid.

21. U.S. Department of Labor, Bureau of Labor Statistics, *Occupational Outlook Handbook,* 1970–71 edition; 1973–74 edition.

22. *Computerworld,* September 3, 1975, p. 4.

23. Ibid.

24. *Computer Manpower Outlook,* p. 3.

25. L. Schwartz and G. Heilbon, "Marketing the Computer," *Datamation* (October 1967), p. 22.

26. See *U.S. Statistical Abstracts,* Science: defense-related expenditures averaged more than 50 per cent of the government total during this period.

27. *Wall Street Journal,* May 12, 1977, p. 40.

28. Reported in *Computerworld,* September 26, 1976, p. 1. From the annual Hansen's Weber Salary Survey. Actually, the salary of all levels of applications programmers increased only 4.6 per cent in the 1976–77 period.

29. Source EDP, "1977 Computer Salary Survey," (Union, N.J.), p. 8. According to this, cost of living jumped 11 per cent in 1974 and another 9 per cent in 1975. It was during those years that data-processing workers (like other workers) received no salary increases, resulting in a marked decline in their real wages.

30. *Computerworld*, September 26, 1976, p. 1.

31. Each year sees an increasing number of data-processing salary surveys. The proliferation of statistics makes it more difficult to compare salaries over several years. Each survey usually breaks the data down by job title, geographic region, size of installation, and type of industry. The Bureau of Labor Statistics, for example, compiles Area Wage Surveys (by geographic region). These statistics report the range and median salaries for each job title as well as differences by sex. In the New York metropolitan region, the 1976 median starting salary for programmers was $230 (about $11,900 annually), and the same figure for operators was $180 ($9,000 annually). Within the data-processing field, the most widely discussed figures are those provided by the annual *Infosystems* (a trade journal) salary survey. These statistics, based on a sample of companies across the country, do not correspond directly to Bureau of Labor Statistics categories, although they do reflect the same trends. In addition to the two sources cited above, Source EDP, an employment agency, and the Hansen's Weber Survey represent two additional salary surveys. Again, they differ in sampling techniques and categories, but the overall range of salaries for each job title is similar in them, as well as the percentages from year to year.

32. Lecht, p. 6. These numbers are widely quoted, although they do seem surprisingly low. The data are based on the concept of a computer *system*, which includes a Central Processing Unit and any number of input/output devices (such as printers, terminals, tapes) attached to it. It does not include the newer microprocessors or small single function computers. The more current figure refers to computer installations or "shops." Many installations maintain more than one computer system.

33. See U.S. Department of Labor, Bureau of Labor Statistics, *Occupational Outlook Handbook*, Bulletin 1875, 1976–77. It is difficult to obtain reliable and consistent figures for the number of data-processing workers because definitions about data-processing work have themselves undergone change. Some sources estimate the current number of data-processing workers to be more than one million, but this considers all workers who *interact* with computer equipment. This study is about only those workers who directly operate, program, and design computer applications in a commercial environment; the 500,000 number is probably more reflective of this population.

34. *Wall Street Journal*, May 12, 1977, p. 40.

35. Philip S. Nyborg, Pender M. McCarter, William Erickson, eds., *Information Processing in the United States, A Quantitative Survey* (Montvale, N.J.: AFIPS Press, 1977).

36. *Computerworld*, August 8, 1977, p. 1. It is important, however, to

consider that while labor costs, *as a share of total costs,* may rise, total data-processing costs are not rising proportionally because hardware costs are declining.

37. Kraft, p. 57.

38. Richard H. Hall, *Occupations and the Social Structure,* 2d ed. (Englewood Cliffs, N.J.: Prentice-Hall, 1975), p. 355.

39. David Noble, *America By Design* (New York: Alfred A. Knopf, 1977), p. xxii, emphasis added. For further discussions about the ways in which people, particularly people organized in groups, interact and affect technology, see Peter F. Drucker, *Technology, Management, and Society* (New York: Harper & Row, 1970), and C. Wright Mills, *White Collar* (New York: Oxford University Press, 1951).

40. A large number of introductory textbooks is devoted to data processing. For the novice who does not want to become an expert, I would recommend Enid Squire, *The Computer: An Everyday Machine,* 2d ed. (Menlo Park, Calif.: Addison-Wesley, 1977), and Stanley Rothman and Charles Mosmann, *Computers and Society* 2d ed. (Chicago: SRA, 1976).

41. See Herman H. Goldstine, *The Computer from Pascal to Von Neuman* (Princeton: Princeton University Press, 1972). Goldstine worked on the development of the first computers. For other histories of the early period, see Margaret Harman, *Stretching Man's Mind, A History of Data Processing* (New York: Mason/Charter, 1975); Alan Vorwald, *Computers from Sand Table to Electronic Brain* (1970), Shirley Thomas, *Computers, their History, Present, and Future* (1965).

42. See Gerald W. Brock, *The U.S. Computer Industry, A Study in Market Power* (Cambridge, Mass.: Ballinger Publishing Co., 1975), Chap. 2. Almost every book written about the computer field includes some brief history of computers and most single out a few heroes who are the supposed "fathers" of computer technology. Recently (1977) the subject of early computer developments has captured the hearts of computer buffs and has even been included in formal professional association conferences. With the new emphasis on the early history have come, of course, conflicting theories on where the laurels should be placed. My own preference is toward recognition of John Atanasoff, who began development of a computer in 1937 at Iowa State College. His machine did not receive much publicity or funding, but its design seems to have been borrowed by John Mauchly after a meeting between them in 1940 (Brock, pp. 9–10). Another group of unsung heroes, or actually heroines, is the team of women who were recruited to do the hand calculations for the ENIAC. These women, most of whom had mathematics or science backgrounds, were employed to develop the software. In essence they are the first programmers (see Goldstine).

43. "Survey and Study of the Computer Field," *Computers and Automation,* January 1963, p. 23.

44. Ibid.

45. Brock, p. 13.

46. Ibid., p. 12.

47. Ibid., p. 12. A "family" of computers is a group of similar machines that vary in size and speed. During this early period each computer was built under special contract and several different memory systems were employed. IBM used a rotating drum in its very popular 650 model, introduced in 1954. The drum allowed little storage or memory space, but it was quite reliable. In their 701 model, IBM used electrostatic cathode-ray memory, which gave more storage capacity but with slightly less reliability. UNIVAC used acoustic delay line memory in its UNIVAC I, which like the IBM 701 memory was larger but less reliable than the 650. The range of competing techniques was indicative of the experimental nature of the first half of the 1950s. No one type of hardware component was considered best in terms of its functional characteristics and no single method had yet been deemed cost efficient.

48. Brock, p. 15.

49. Ibid.

50. Ibid., pp. 18–20. See also testimony from *U.S. vs IBM*, for evidence supporting these points.

51. Charles Lecht, *Waves of Change* (New York: Advanced Computer Techniques, 1977), p. 13. It is difficult to define a "comparable" machine in both 1950 and 1970 terms. These figures refer to decreasing hardware costs and increasing hardware capability. Expressed yet another way, the cost per 100,000 computations decreased from $1.26 in 1952 to 5¢ in 1977. The numbers do not directly take labor and software costs into account.

52. R. L. Patrick, "Ten Years of Progress?" *Datamation*, September 1967, p. 23. For a more detailed history of software see Jean Sammet, *Programming Languages: History and Fundamentals* (Englewood Cliffs, N.J.: Prentice-Hall, 1969). Systems software is composed of groups of programs that act as "super programs" to direct the processing of application or user programs. The purpose of system software is to increase the efficiency of the system—including hardware efficiency (throughput) as well as labor efficiency.

53. George F. Weinwurm, ed., *On the Management of Computer Programming* (Philadelphia: Auerbach Publishers, 1970), p. xiv.

54. IBM called its 360 operating system, The Operating System. This has, of course, made the general term into an IBM product name.

55. Frederick P. Brooks, Jr., *The Mythical Man-Month* (Reading, Mass.: Addison-Wesley, 1975), p. viii.

Chapter 3

1. For perhaps the best-known treatment of this theme, see Alfred Dupont Chandler, *Strategy and Structure*, 2d ed. (Garden City, N.Y.: Anchor Books, 1966).

2. Douglas McGregor, *The Human Side of Enterprise* (New York: McGraw-Hill, 1960).

3. Ibid., pp. 3–4, emphasis added.

4. Ernest Dale, *Management: Theory and Practice* 3d ed. (New York: McGraw-Hill, 1973). See also Harry Braverman, *Labor and Monopoly Capital* (New York: Monthly Review Press, 1974), for a detailed history of Scientific Management; and Frederick W. Taylor, *The Principles of Scientific Management* (New York: Harper and Row, 1947).

5. Many, including Taylor, have felt that Scientific Management was never implemented. Thirty years after its introduction, Taylor argued that not a single company had fully adopted his techniques for Scientific Management, although the mechanics of time-motion study had indeed caught on (see Dale, p. 124). Today more than a half-century after his first experiments there can be little doubt that the key elements of Taylor's ideas still dominate management theory. The issue concerning their *use*, however, raises the question of whether his principles were ever successful. For a more detailed analysis of Scientific Management and the problems that surrounded it, see Braverman, pp. 85–137; see also David Noble, *America by Design: Science, Technology, and the Rise of Corporate Capitalism* (New York: Alfred A. Knopf, 1976). For discussions about the implementation of Taylor's principles, see Brian Palmer, "Class, Conception & Conflict: The Thrust of Efficiency, Managerial Views of Labor and Working Class Rebellion, 1903–1922," *Review of Radical Political Economics* 7, no. 2 (Summer 1975), pp. 31–49. In particular, the issues are summarized by Maarten de Kadt, "The Importance of Distinguishing between Levels of Generalities," *RRPE* 8 no. 3 (Fall 1976), pp. 65–67.

6. Hugh G. J. Aitken, *Taylorism at the Watertown Arsenal, Scientific Management in Action 1905–1915* (Cambridge: Harvard University Press, 1960), p. 135.

7. Peter F. Drucker, *The Practice of Management* (New York, 1954), p. 280.

8. Aitken, pp. 200–211.

9. Douglas McGregor, "Perspectives on Organization and the Manager's Role," in *Management Organization and the Computer,* George P. Shultz, Thomas L. Whisler, eds. (Glencoe, Ill.: Free Press, 1960), p. 101.

10. Mike Hales, "Management Science and the Second Industrial Revolution," *Radical Science Journal,* 1 (January 1974), p. 13.

11. For more detail from a management perspective on the Hawthorne Studies, see Dale; for a more precise analysis of the "Hawthorne effect," see Maarten de Kadt, "The Development of Management Structures, the Problems of the Control of Workers in Large Corporations" (Ph.D. dissertation, New School for Social Research, 1976), pp. 78–82.

12. These concerns were even addressed in Taylor's day by Lillian Gilbreth, who working with her husband Frank on applications of time-motion efficiency, began to realize that workers needed more than straight financial reward. Lillian Gilbreth's contributions broadened the scope of incentive schemes, opening the door to concepts of worker welfare.

13. Probably the literature from the Harvard Business School best typifies the emphasis on these terms. Almost any issue of the *Harvard Business Review* contains articles on allocating or controlling human resources. For books that spell out the application of these terms, see Rensis Likert, *The Human Organization* (New York: McGraw-Hill, 1967), and Chris Argyris, *Integrating the Individual and the Organization* (New York: John Wiley and Sons, 1964), as well as Douglas McGregor, *The Human Side of Enterprise.*

14. de Kadt, "Development of Management Structures," p. 53.

15. Some have called this the "Integrationist School" because it merges so many disciplines. It is important to remember that management science does not exist as a unified theory, but represents, rather, a collection of theories and techniques pointed toward solving problems associated with "allocating business resources." Drucker tells us that it is a philosophy, and indeed it is that, more than a science. Within its literature there are many contrasting points of view, unified however in their objectives. See Edward A. Tomeski, *The Computer Revolution, The Executive and the New Information Technology* (New York: Macmillan Co., 1970); Peter F. Drucker, *Technology, Management, and Society* (New York: Harper and Row, 1970).

16. Drucker, *Technology, Management, and Society,* p. 193. See also C. West Churchman. *The Systems Approach* (New York: Delacorte Press, 1968).

17. Ibid., p. 193.

18. Hales, p. 23.

19. Herbert A. Simon, *The Shape of Automation for Men and Management* (New York: Harper Torchbooks, 1965), pp. 58–76.

20. In his essay on management science, Hales calls this "the fetishism of measurement in cash terms" (p. 7). His terminology grows out of the Marxian category of fetishism of commodities, which simply stated means that since under capitalism all commodities are produced for exchange, the essence of each commodity is the measurement of its exchange value in the market. Viewed in this light, it becomes clear that measuring each "resource" in the production process includes measurement of the thoughts and actions of workers. Part II of this study will look at the ways this fetishism interferes with worker productivity.

21. See Churchman.

22. See Chandler.

23. McGregor, *The Human Side of Enterprise,* p. 3.

24. Argyris p. 60. He agrees that "unintended consequences" can arise from management policy when there is a "lack of congruency between individual needs and organizational demands." These results in "antagonistic adoptive activities" such as aggression, "goldbricking," absenteeism, and slowdowns. In other words, dissatisfied workers resist management orders resulting in unproductive work!

25. For general discussions concerning "labor/management conflicts," see management textbooks such as Dale, and systems develop-

ment literature; for example: Robert M. Gagne, ed., *Psychological Principles in System Development* (New York: Holt, Rinehart, and Winston, 1962).

26. These categories are presented as analytical tools to help focus management perceptions in the light of labor process changes. Management literature does not use these specific categories, but I found them useful in order to abstract the motives and direction of labor process change from the operational policies defined in the literature.

27. See, for example, L. G. Wagner, "Computers, Decentralization and Corporate Control," in William F. Boore, Jerry R. Murphy, eds., *The Computer Sampler: Management Perspectives on the Computer* (New York: McGraw-Hill, 1968), for computer operations research techniques. Also see Gagne for the use of systems analysis in decision-making, and Robert Boguslaw, *The New Utopians: A Study of Systems Design and Social Change* (Englewood Cliffs, N.J.: Prentice-Hall, 1965).

28. David Hickson, D. S. Pugh, Diana C. Pheysey, "Operations, Technology and Organization Structure," *Administrative Science Quarterly* 14, no. 3, (September 1969), pp. 378–397.

29. In the data-processing field this view is probably best characterized by the writings of Dick Brandon, who argues that data-processing workers, particularly programmers, are in need of constant managerial control. See Dick H. Brandon, *Management Standards for Data Processing* (New York: Van Nostrand, 1963), and *Management Planning for Data Processing* (New York: Brandon Systems Press, 1970).

30. For examples of management theory that lean toward McGregor's theory Y school, see Argyris, Likert, and Carl B. Kauffman, *Man Incorporate, the Individual and His Work in an Organized Society* (Garden City, N.Y.: Doubleday, 1967). In the data-processing field Gerald Weinberg is an outspoken advocate of "humanistic" management. See Gerald M. Weinberg, *The Psychology of Computer Programming* (New York: Van Nostrand Reinhold, 1971).

31. See, for example, James March and Herbert A. Simon, *Organization* (New York: John Wiley and Sons, 1958).

32. Dale, p. 149.

33. See Chandler.

34. Centralized organization structure focuses most important decision-making within the central or top management of the firm. Decentralized structure allows for units or divisions of a firm to be responsible for some predefined decisions. Matrix management, while still evolving, allows for some flexibility by mixing some of the elements of both centralized and decentralized structures. See De Kadt, "Development of Management Structure."

35. Drucker, *Management Technology and Society,* pp. 112–114.

36. George F. Weinwurm, "The Challenge to the Management Community," in *On the Management of Computer Programming* (Philadelphia: Auerbach Publishers, 1970), pp. 235–38.

37. In particular see Drucker, *Management, Technology, and Society.*

38. See the literature on "technology transfer," which outlines the procedures involved in transferring defense-related technology to private industry; for example, Samuel I. Doctors, *The Role of Federal Agencies in Technology Transfer* (Cambridge: MIT Press, 1969).

39. Drucker, *Management, Technology, and Society*, p. 48.

40. Ibid. p. 32.

41. Management, like any other discipline or science, tends to get puffed up on its own importance and exaggerates its role in relation to all else. Nevertheless, this chapter attempts to portray the objectives and methods of management theory as *perceived* by the theorists. What happens in practice is influenced by these writings—egocentric or not.

42. This section is by no means a survey of all radical theory about labor. It focuses only on those theories that describe the labor *process* and ignores the large body of literature that characterizes the factors involved in shaping the labor *market*. It also excludes a discussion of the labor theory of value, which—although it would be illustrative of the larger agruments in this study—would be too encompassing to attempt here. There is, however, a central argument in both labor market theory and the labor theory of value that bears mentioning: Within the capitalist system of exchange, all "resources" are treated as commodities—that is, they can be bought and sold on the market for quantifiable sums. Thus labor, in capitalist terms, is a commodity—a thing. See Karl Marx, *Capital*, Vol. I (New York: International Publishers, 1974), Chap. 1.

43. David M. Gordon, "Capitalist Efficiency and Socialist Efficiency," *Monthly Review* 28, no. 3 (July-August 1976), pp. 19–39. See also Stanley Arnowitz, "Marx, Technology, and Labor" (Ph.D. dissertation, Union Graduate School, 1975).

44. Daniel Bell, *The Cultural Contradictions of Capitalism* (New York: Basic Books, 1976), p. 11.

45. See Laird Cummings and Joan Greenbaum, "The Struggle over Productivity: Workers, Management and Technology," in *U.S. Capitalism in Crisis*, Union for Radical Political Economics, January 1978. The basis for this distinction is found in Karl Marx, *Capital*, Vol. I, P. II, Chap. 6. See also Herbert Gintis, "The Nature of the Labor Exchange and the Theory of Capitalist Production." *RRPE* 8, no. 2 (Summer 1976), pp. 36–52. Gintis put the issue quite simply: "The neoclassical theory of production is based on the crucial assumption that the labor exchange (the social process whereby the worker exchanges his or her labor for a wage) can be treated solely as an exchange of commodities" (p. 40); "This basic neoclassical fallacy is *precisely* the blurring of the distinction between labor and labor-power" (p. 42).

46. Stephen Marglin, "What do Bosses Do? The Origins and Functions of Hierarchy in Capitalist Production," *RRPE* 6, no. 2 (Summer 1974), pp. 33–60, and Marglin's unpublished "Postscript Notes," 1975. For an analysis of Marglin's arguments, see Laird Cummings, "The Rationalization and Automation of Clerical Work" (Master's thesis, Brooklyn College, School of Social Science, May 1977).

See also Andrew L. Friedman, *Industry and Labour, Class Struggle at Work and Monopoly Capitalism* (London: Macmillan, 1977), for an excellent history and case study of management strategies and their interactions with worker resistance.

47. Harry Braverman, *Labor and Monopoly Capital, The Degradation of Work in the Twentieth Century* (New York: Monthly Review Press, 1975), pp. 72–73.

48. Karl Marx, *Capital,* I, p. 178.

49. Ibid., p. 363.

50. Braverman, pp. 113, 114, 119.

51. Richard C. Edwards, "The Social Relations of Production in the Firm and Labor Market Structure," in Richard C. Edwards, Michael Reich, and David M. Gordon, eds., *Labor Market Segmentation* (Lexington, Mass.: D. C. Heath, 1975), p. 11

52. Ibid., pp. 11–12. See also Edward's "Alienation and Inequality: Capitalist Relations of Production in Bureaucratic Enterprises" (Ph.D. dissertation, Harvard University, July 1972), for an expanded discussion of these modes of compliance.

53. See Samuel Bowles and Herbert Gintis, *Schooling in Capitalist America, Educational Reform and the Contradictions of Economic Life* (New York: Basic Books, 1976).

54. Jeremy Brecher and Tim Costello, *Common Sense for Hard Times* (New York: Two Continents Press; Washington, D.C.: Institute for Policy Studies, 1976), p. 52. Katherine Stone found the same mechanisms operative in the steel industry. She argues that at the turn of the century "the establishment of a job ladder had two advantages, from the employers' point of view. First, it gave workers a sense of vertical mobility as they made their way up the ladder, and was an incentive to workers to work harder. . . . The other advantage of job ladder arrangement was that it gave the employers more leverage with which to maintain discipline." See Katherine Stone, "The Origins of Job Structures in the Steel Industry," *RRPE* 6, no. 2 (Summer 1974), p. 74.

55. Brecher and Costello, p. 52. Also Peter B. Doeringer and Michael J. Piore, *Internal Labor Markets and Manpower Analysis* (Lexington, Mass.: Heath Lexington Books, 1971), describe the creation of what they call "internal labor markets" within the firm. These structures such as job ladders, points of entry, and patterns of promotion are handles with which management can control entry, exist, and mobility within the enterprise.

56. See Marglin and Braverman.

57. In Ernest Dale, *Management Theory and Practice,* 3d ed. (New York: McGraw-Hill, 1973), p. 159; see Weber's essay "Bureaucracy," pp. 196–244, in H. H. Gerth and C. Wright Mills, *From Max Weber: Essays in Sociology* (New York: Oxford University Press, 1946).

58. Edwards, in *Labor Market Segmentation,* pp. 9–10, emphasis added.

59. See Edwards, "Alienation and Inequality"; see also Laird

Cummings, "Rationalization and Automation." In his study of clerical workers in a large insurance company, Cummings finds that the impersonal aura gives workers the feeling that management is neither "harsh" nor "blatant." Workers interviewed who are about to lose their jobs as a result of a new computer system point out their feelings that it's not the fault of their boss, but just the way the "system" works.

60. Brecher and Costello, p. 45, emphasis added.

61. Nathan Rosenberg, "Marx as a Student of Technology," *Monthly Review* 28, no. 3 (July-August 1976), p. 70.

62. Karl Marx, *The Poverty of Philosophy* (Moscow, n.d.) p. 105, in Rosenberg, p. 74.

63. David Noble, *America by Design* (New York: Alfred A. Knopf, 1977), p. xix.

64. The impact of computer and information technology on current business strategies is well beyond the scope of this study. I introduce the topic here because it is useful for getting a better focus on the tasks done by data-processing workers.

65. Edward A. Tomeski, *The Computer Revolution* (New York: Macmillan Co., 1970), p. 10.

66. Warren Alberts, "Case Study: Air Lines," in George P. Shultz, and Thomas L. Wisler, eds., *Management Organization and the Computer* (Glencoe, Ill.: Free Press, 1960), p. 177.

67. C. Wright Mills, *White Collar* (New York: Oxford University Press, 1951), p. 192–193. Emphasis added.

68. Shultz and Whisler, p. 7.

69. Thomas L. Whisler, "The Impact of Information Technology on Organizational Control," in Charles A. Myers, ed., *The Impact of Computers on Management* (Cambridge: MIT Press, 1967), pp. 16–39. For an analysis of these effects from a sociological perspective, see Richard H. Hall, *Occupations and the Social Structure*, 2d ed. (Englewood Cliffs, N.J.: Prentice-Hall, 1975), Chap. 11.

70. L. G. Wagner, "Computers, Decentralization and Corporate Control," in William F. Boor and Jerry R. Murphy, eds., *The Computer Sampler: Management Perspectives on the Computer* (New York: McGraw-Hill, 1968), pp. 106–8.

71. Ibid., p. 106.

72. Maarten de Kadt, "The Development of Management Structures, the Problems of the Control of Workers in Large Corporations" (Ph.D. dissertation, New School for Social Research, 1976).

73. Shultz and Whisler, p. xiii.

74. Herbert A. Simon, "Management and Decision-Making," in Irene Traviss, ed., *The Computer Impact* (Englewood Cliffs, N.J.: Prentice-Hall, 1970), p. 63. See Herbert A. Simon, *The Shape of Automation for Men and Management* (New York: Harper Torchbooks, 1965), for an in-depth study of structure of management decision-making and the relationship of automation to decision-making rules.

75. The term "data-processing management literature" covers the

ground from theoretical essays to "how-to-manage" articles in trade publications. At the more theoretical end of the pole, the following books focus on the theme of rationalizing work processes: Charles Lecht, *The Management of Computer Programming Projects* (New York: American Management Association, 1967); Frederick P. Brooks, Jr., *The Mythical Man-Month, Essays on Software Engineering* (Reading, Mass.: Addison-Wesley, 1975); Robert G. Canning and Roger L. Sisson, *The Management of Data Processing* (New York: John Wiley and Sons, 1967). See also George F. Weinwurm, ed., *On The Management of Computer Programming* (Philadelphia: Auerbach Publishers, 1970); and Dick Brandon, *Management Standards for Data Processing* (New York: Van Nostrand, 1963).

76. Probably the best summary of these arguments can be found in George F. Weinwurm, "The Challenge to the Management Community," in *On the Management of Computer Programming.*

77. This argument runs throughout the history of data-processing work. It is still being aired today in conferences and trade publications. For an example of management's statement of the issue, see Carl H. Reynolds, "What's Wrong with Computer Programming Management," in Weinwurm, ed., *On the Management.*

78. Weinwurm, "The Challenge to the Management Community," p. 235.

79. "Unlocking the Computer Profit Potential," McKinsey and Co. report (1968), in Stanley Rothman and Charles Mossman, *Computers and Sociaty,* 2d ed. (Chicago: SRA, 1976), p. 196.

80. See Robert J. Canning and Roger L. Sisson, *The Management of Data Processing,* pp. 12–15.

81. David Noble, *America By Design* (New York: Alfred A. Knopf, 1977).

82. Reinhard Bendix, *Work and Authority in Industry* (Berkeley and Los Angeles: University of California Press, 1956), p. 13.

Chapter 4

1. Dick Brandon, "The Economics of Computer Programming," in George F. Weinwurm, ed., *On the Management of Computer Programming* (Philadelphia: Auerbach Publishers, 1970), p. 8.

2. Philip Kraft, *Programmers and Managers* (New York: Springer-Verlag, 1977), in particular Chap. 3.

3. See Philip S. Nyborg, and Pender M. McCarter, William Erickson, eds. *Information Processing in the United States, a Quantitative Survey* (Montvale, N.J.: AFIPS Press, 1977).

4. The material in this and the following chapter relies heavily on the interviews I conducted for this study. Where applicable, I interweave the interview material with other data sources. All too often, particularly in the case of computer operators, comparative data sources were not available.

5. Andrew M. Pettigrew, "Occupational Specialization as an Emergent Process," *The Sociological Review* 21, no. 2 (May 1973), p. 262.

6. Continuously since the early 1960s, trade publications have carried a series of management "complaint" articles about data-processing workers' behavior. In the 1960s the most widely read trade publications included *Datamation, Business Automation,* and *Computers and Automation.* In addition *Computerworld,* the weekly industry newspaper, reports on conferences, seminars, and business reports in which these complaints are aired.

7. Karl Marx, *Capital,* Vol. I (New York: International Publishers, 1967), p. 362.

8. Pettigrew, p. 262.

9. Herbert Simon, "Management and Decision-Making," in Irene Traviss, ed., *The Computer Impact* (Englewood Cliffs, N.J.: Prentice-Hall, 1970), pp. 59–68.

10. Marshall Meyer, "Automation and Bureaucratic Structure," *American Journal of Sociology* 74, no. 3 (1968), pp. 256–264. See also Peter M. Blau, "The Hierarchy of Authority in Organizations," *American Journal of Sociology* 73, no. 4 (January 1968), pp. 453–467.

11. Pettigrew, p. 265.

12. Ibid., p. 267.

13. Ibid., p. 262.

14. See George F. Weinwurm, ed., *On the Management of Computer Programming* (Philadelphia: Auerbach Publishers, 1970), for a collection of articles on this subject. Today the issue of data-processing work standards is continually addressed in the following trade publications: *Data Management, Datamation, Computers and People* (formerly Computers and Automation), and *Infosystems* (formerly *Business Automation*). The literature of the American Federation of Information Processing Societies (AFIPS) and the Data Processing Management Association (DPMA) cover the spectrum on management control standards. Although both organizations represent management, their publications include both humanistic or "soft-line" methods as well as more authoritarian strategies. The "how-to-manage" articles in the data-processing trade magazines, as well as the management technique books cited elsewhere in this chapter, are literally filled with reports on the "successful" way to subdivide and define tasks. Edward Nelson, for example details thirty-six tasks in the programming process and emphasizes the need to quantify and measure each step for time and performance ("Some Recent Contributions to Computer Programming Management," in Weinwurm, ed., *On the Management*). All programming projects, regardless of size or function, have the same sequence of tasks: defining the problem, flowcharting, coding, testing, documenting, and operating. Each one can be subdivided into smaller units: for example, testing is made up of unit testing (each program is tested), system integration testing (the programs in the system are run together), and parallel testing (the system is tried with actual data and the results are compared to the former processing method).

15. George F. Weinwurm, "On the Economic Analysis of Computer Programming," in *On the Management,* pp. 187–216. The list of formulae for calculating productivity rates is almost endless, although they all vary around the same theme. Weinwurm's Production Rate, for example, is typical:

$$\frac{\text{\# of Machine Instructions delivered}}{\text{Man-months for program design, code, and testing}}$$

16. National Conference on Computer Systems Productivity, Capitol Area Chapter, Society for Management Information Systems, Washington, D.C., June 27–29, 1977.

17. R. L. Patrick, "Ten Years of Progress?" *Datamation,* September 1967, pp. 22, 23. The terms "idle time," and "set-up time" refer to that time when the computer may not be in use because the operator is preparing (setting up) another job. "Re-run" time refers to those times when the run was unsuccessful (programmer, operator or machine problem) and must be tried again.

18. Ibid., p. 23.

19. Kraft, p. 97.

20. Patrick, p. 23.

21. Kraft, p. 55.

22. Ibid., p. 58.

23. In Phillip S. Nyborg, Pender M. McCarter, and William Erickson, *Information Processing in the United States: A Quantitative Study* (Montvale, N.J.: AFIPS Press, 1977); T. B. Steel, Jr., "A Note on Future Trends," p. 48.

24. Adam Smith, *The Wealth of Nations,* quoted in Andrew Zimbalist, "The Limits of Work Humanization," *RRPE* 7, no. 2 (Summer 1975), p. 51.

Chapter 5

1. Herb Grosch made this statement to me at the National Conference on Computer Systems Productivity, sponsored by the Capital Area Chapter of the Society for Management Informations Systems, Washington, D.C., June 28, 1977.

2. It's certainly clear that many workers have been changed by the economic crisis of the early 1970s, but the changes among data-processing workers are more pronounced. It's as if twenty or thirty years of corporate behavioral modification has been compressed into ten for data-processing workers.

3. "A Profile of the Programmer," a study by Deutsch and Shea, Inc. (New York: Industrial Relations News, 1963), p. 17. This early study appears to be the only in-depth investigation of programmer background, goals, and values. A representative of the firm, now called Deutsch, Shea, and Evans, said that the company has published another

survey, *Profile of the EDP Professional.* See also Dallis Perry and William Cannon, "Vocational Interests of Computer Programmers," *Journal of Applied Psychology* 51, no. 1 (February 1967), pp. 28–34, for a report on programmer interests using the Strong Vocational Interest Blank. Both studies found that most programmers did not choose data processing, but rather "ended up" in it after trying other things. It is interesting to note that Perry and Cannon used the SVIB on a sample of men since they were interested in developing a "key," and it was felt that women's interests might be different. The following year they conducted the profiles on a group of women programmers and found the results to be similar. They were particularly struck with the fact that women, too, seemed to prefer independent nonroutine work! "Vocational Interest of Female Programmers," *Journal of Applied Psychology* 52 (1968), pp. 31-35.

4. Joseph Weizenbaum, *Computer Power and Human Reason* (New York: W. H. Freeman, 1976), p. 116.

5. Dick Brandon, "The Economics of Computer Programming," in George Weinwurm, ed., *On the Management of Computer Programming* (Philadelphia: Auerbach Publishers, 1970), pp. 10–11. Brandon expands on these characteristics at some length. In the 1960s he found a "greater incidence of beards, sandals and other symbols of rugged individualism or nonconformity," and urged better selection techniques to weed out this problem. His concern was that although the aptitude tests used for selection look for logical abilities, "this is often not supported by maturity or reasoned thinking ability . . . [and] because the programmer has absolute control over his product and his productivity, his incapacity for mature cooperation with management can prevent effective control."

6. Andrew M. Pettigrew, "Occupational Specialization as an Emergent Process," *The Sociological Review* 21, no. 2 (May 1973), pp. 255–278.

7. The Programmer Aptitude Test is an IBM-inspired measurement tool that, despite its many critics, is still in widespread use. Other tests include the Wonderlic Personnel Test and the Primary Mental Abilities Test.

8. Gerald M. Weinberg, *The Psychology of Computer Programming* (New York: Van Nostrand Reinhold, 1971), p. 155, emphasis added.

9. Ibid., pp. 148–152. It's ironic that a humanist like Weinberg gets caught in his own trap. Although he criticizes managers for their harsh and authoritarian treatment of programmers, his list of ideal characteristics would not be easy to accomplish. No wonder programmers need a strong sense of humor—how else could they balance humility with assertiveness and tolerance of stress with neatness!

10. David Mayer and Ashford W. Stalnaker, "Selection and Evaluation of Computer Personnel," in Weinwurm, p. 138.

11. Mark McColloch, "White Collar Electrical Machinery, Banking, and Public Welfare Workers 1940–1970" (Ph.D. dissertation, University of Pittsburgh, 1975), pp. 108, 109.

12. Jack Stone, "The Human Connection," *Computerworld,* July 4, 1977, p. 17.

13. See Richard C. Edwards, "The Social Relations of Production in the Firm and Labor Market Structure," in Richard C. Edwards, Michael Reich, David M. Gordon, eds., *Labor Market Segmentation* (Lexington, Mass.: D. C. Heath, 1975), pp. 3–26.

14. Peter F. Drucker, *The Age of Discontinuity, Guidelines to Our Changing Society* (New York: Harper and Row, 1968), p. 59.

15. Philip Kraft, *Programmers and Managers, the Routinization of Computer Programming in the United States* (New York: Springer-Verlag, 1977), p. 36.

16. See, for example, Gloria M. Silvern, "Programmed Instruction for Computer Programming," *Computers and Automation,* March 1963, pp. 12–18; and James Rogers and Donald Bullock, "The Application of Programmed Instruction in the Computer Field," *Computers and Automation,* April 1963, pp. 22–25.

17. CAI involves the "student/worker" sitting at a computer terminal and being drilled and quizzed via a series of preprogrammed instructions. The information presented is very cut and dried and usually extremely detailed. Film loops do the same kind of thing but graphically; often they are used in conjunction with CAI and PIs for testing purposes.

18. Annual Survey, *Infosystems* 19, no. 7 (July 1972), pp. 44–46.

19. See, for example, "Education: No Interface from Campus to Corporation," *Infosystems* 21, June 1974, p. 34. For further discussion on this issue see the annual Proceedings of the Association for Computing Machinery (semiannual in the 1960s) (ACM) and the American Federation of Information Processing Societies (AFIPS). The ACM publishes updated curriculum guidelines for computer science degree programs.

20. See Perry and Cannon, "Vocational Interests of Computer Programming."

21. By 1969, after mounting government pressure, IBM began a policy of "separate pricing"—that is, they charged independent prices for hardware, software, and education. The government had forced the issue, claiming that the IBM policy of free education to customers was a monopolistic practice. The argument that educational credentials are an important "screening" device is made by economists of the human capital school. Formal schooling rather than on-the-job training shifts the investment in human capital from the employer to the potential worker. In particular see Joseph E. Stiglitz, "The Theory of 'Screening,' Education, and the Distribution of Income," *American Economic Review,* June 1975, pp. 283–300. See also Jacob Mincer, "On-The-Job Training Costs, Returns, and Some Implications," in John F. Burton, Jr. et al., eds., *Readings in Labor Market Analysis* (New York: Holt, Rinehart, and Winston, 1971), pp. 201–230.

22. Reported in *Computerworld,* June 27, 1977, p. 18.

23. Edwards. p. 9.

24. Jeremy Brecher and Tim Costello, *Common Sense for Hard Times* (New York: Two Continents Press; Washington: Institute for Policy Studies, 1976), p. 50.

25. Marshall Meyer, "Automation and Bureaucratic Structure," *American Journal of Sociology* 74, no. 3 (November 1968), pp. 256–264.

26. For definitions of data-processing job titles, see *The Occupational Outlook Handbook,* annual, Bureau of Labor Statistics, as well as other BLS publications, such as the Area Wage Surveys. In addition, see *Infosystem* (formerly *Business Automation*) annual salary review issue.

27. Kraft, p. 81. Chap. 5 of Kraft's book has an excellent description of the management functions of career ladders.

28. See Richard E. Weber and Bruce Gilchrist, "Discrimination in the Employment of Women in the Computer Industry," *Communications of the ACM* 18, no. 7 (July 1975), pp. 416–418. See also "National Survey of Professional, Administrative, Technical and Clerical Pay," U.S. Dept. of Labor, 1976. See Kraft, Chap. 2. In addition, the patterns of discrimination that I mention are based on my own experiences and those of the people I interviewed.

29. Pettigrew, p. 263.

30. Ernest Dale, *Management Theory and Practice* (New York: McGraw-Hill, 1973), p. 356.

31. Michael Maccoby, *The Gamesman, The New Corporate Leaders* (New York: Simon and Shuster, 1976), p. 100.

32. See Kraft, Chap. 5.

33. Reported in *Computerworld,* Dec. 17, 1976, p. 12.

34. *Computerworld,* October 18, 1976, p. 17. *Computerworld* regularly reports on the issues of licensing of data-processing workers. In addition it provides extensive coverage on the data-processing societies and the "professional" interests that concern them. The Institute for Certification of Computer Professionals now offers two examinations—the CDP for "Candidates . . . [having] a professional attitude, and a minimum of sixty months full-time . . . work experience," and the CCP, Certificate in Computer Programming "intended for senior-level programmers." Brochures for these examinations are available from the Institute for Certification of Computer Professionals.

35. "Even Babysitters Have to Eat," *Datamation,* May 1974, p. 111.

36. Ibid.

37. It is interesting to note that the issue of professionalism has faded a little faster in England, where white-collar unions are having great success in attracting dp workers. Of an estimated dp workforce of 200,000 union membership is held by 77,000 (*Computerworld,* November 29, 1976).

38. Miles Benson, in *Computerworld,* June 20, 1977, p. 34, and June 27, 1977, p. 14.

39. David M. Gordon, "Capitalist Efficiency & Socialist Efficiency," *Monthly Review* 28, no. 3 (July-August 1976), pp. 19–39.

40. Management confuses the issues of supply and demand when it

comes to people. When managers argue that data-processing workers were in short supply they are really talking about their demand for data-processing labor. They have so structured the demand that an appropriate "supply" would, of course, be hard to find.

Dick Brandon, however, believes that the job characteristics can be (in fact are) so structured that there is little "supply" problem. Brandon lists the required characteristics for operators, programmers, and systems analysts and concludes that: operators could be selected out of the random working population at a ratio of one in two, programmers could be selected from one in every fifteen, and systems analysts could come from a ratio of one analyst to every one hundred (narrowed to college population, this would be one in ten). Brandon's "demands" have so structured the jobs that there is little "supply" problem. *Management Planning for Data Processing* (New York: Brandon Systems Press, 1970), pp. 171–182.

41. Herb Grosch, a self-proclaimed "humanist" complains that today "the cream of the crop are gone," and the field is "filled with a vast number of slobs"! (Interview, Washington, D.C., June 1977, see note 1).

Chapter 6

1. Jeremy Brecher and Tim Costello, *Common Sense For Hard Times* (New York: Two Continents Press; Washington D.C.: Institute for Policy Studies, 1976), p. 42.

2. See Richard C. Edwards, "Alienation and Inequality: Capitalist Relations of Production in Bureaucratic Enterprise" (Ph.D. dissertation, Harvard University, July 1972).

3. Richard H. Hall, *Occupations and the Social Structures,* 2d ed. (Englewood Cliffs, N.J.: Prentice-Hall, 1975), p. 344.

4. The study of bureaucratic organization is as popular in the social sciences as it is in management literature. Peter Blau, for example, has written extensively about hierarchy and authority. His perspective criticizes Max Weber for failing to take note of the existence of informal structures, and thus failing to explore the origins of bureaucracy. I found it interesting Blau trips himself up on the same issue. His studies investigate change within structures, but ignore the creation and function of bureaucracy itself. In particular, see "The Hierarchy of Authority in Organizations," *American Journal of Sociology,* 73, 4, January 1968, pp. 453–467; and *The Dynamics of Bureaucracy* (Chicago: University of Chicago Press, 1963).

5. The origin of hierarchical structure seems to be the military. Some say it has evolved from the Roman armies and others trace its roots to the Austrian army system.

6. See George P. Schultz and Thomas Whisler, eds., *Management Organization and the Computer* (Glencoe, Ill.: Free Press, 1960). See also

Herbert Simon "Management and Decision-Making." in Irene Traviss, ed. *The Computer Impact* (Englewood Cliffs, N.J.: Prentice-Hall, 1970).

7. Richard C. Edwards, "The Social Relations of Production in the Firm and Labor Market Structure," in Richard C. Edwards, Michael Reich, David M. Gordon, eds., *Labor Market Segmentation* (Lexington, Mass.: D. C. Heath, 1975), pp. 9–10.

8. See, for example, Peter Blau and Marshall Meyer, *Bureaucracy in Modern Society* 2d ed. (New York: Random House, 1971); and Marshall Meyer, "Automation and the Bureaucratic Structure," *American Journal of Sociology* 74, no. 3 (November 1968), pp. 256–264.

9. Meyer, "Automation and the Bureaucratic Structure," p. 256.

10. Blau, "The Hierarchy of Authority in Organizations," p. 455.

11. Peter F. Drucker, *Technology, Management, and Society* (New York: Harper and Row, 1970), p. 37.

12. Ibid., p. 37.

13. David Noble, *America By Design* (New York: Alfred A. Knopf, 1977). See also Philip Kraft, *Programmers and Managers* (New York: Springer-Verlag, 1977).

14. Many large programming projects, such as the airline reservation system and electronic funds transfer, have been known to last for a decade or more. The average project length seems to be around six months to one year.

15. Gerald M. Weinberg, *The Psychology of Computer Programming* (New York: Van Nostrand Reinhold, 1971). In particular, see chaps. 4, 5, 6.

16. In software houses and service bureaus (companies that provide programming "products") many projects require programmers to leave the bureau and go "on-site" to the company that requests their service. For service bureau management this causes a problem because they may not get to see "their employee" for several months. The companies that request the service often demand "on-site" programming so that they can actually see the programmer working.

17. Weinberg, p. 108.

18. Frederick P. Brooks, Jr., *The Mythical Man-Month, Essays on Software Engineering* (Reading, Mass.: Addison-Wesley, 1975).

19. In Brooks, Chap. 3. For more information on chief programmer teams, see F. T. Baker, "Chief Programmer Team Management of Production Programming," *IBM Systems Journal* 11. no. 1 (1972). See Kraft, pp. 59–61, for a discussion of the division of labor within chief programmer teams.

Chief programmer team organization bears a similarity to matrix management structure, in that the unitary chain of command is broken and job *functions* become more important than formal fixed organization structure. See William C. Goggin, "How Multi-dimensional Structure Works at Dow Corning," *Harvard Business Review,* 52, no. 1 (January-February 1974), pp. 54–65; for a description of matrix management in action, also see Gerald R. DeMagged, "Matrix Management," *Datamation,* 15, no. 13 (October 15, 1970), pp. 46–49.

20. Brooks, p. 80.

21. Ibid., p. 50.

22. Ibid., p. 44.

23. Ibid., pp. 78–79, emphasis in the original.

24. Meyer, "Automation and the Bureaucratic Structure," pp. 256–264.

Chapter 7

1. I am reminded of one particular technology that did not seem to meet management objectives for controlling the labor process. In the sixties, I worked on preliminary market tests for a mobile computer terminal that worked as a "writing tablet." The tablet was small and fairly portable and would accept hand-printing, which meant that it could be used by anyone. It had been successful in its laboratory tests and had a high degree of reliability. In other words, it was technically possible. Yet the product has never been taken off the laboratory shelf. Almost all terminal-based communication today is dependent on typewriter devices; the exceptions are the optical product code scanners, mark sense devices, and now some voice grade units; devices that require codified data and/or controllable stationary situations. IBM felt that the results of its market tests showed that industry was not "interested" in a device such as the "writing tablet."

2. For a discussion of clerical costs in banking, see Mark McColloch, "White-Collar Electrical Machinery, Banking and Public Welfare Workers 1940–1970" (Ph.D. dissertation, University of Pittsburgh, 1975). For a discussion of increasing clerical costs in the insurance industry, see Laird Cummings, "The Rationalization and Automation of Clerical Work" (Master's thesis, Brooklyn College, May 1977).

3. The advertisements for software packages illustrate that the *biggest* feature is the *replacement* of clerical labor costs. Of course the packages rarely perform the way the advertisements say they will.

4. See Bureau of Labor Statistics for general figures on the increase in the number of service sector jobs. See also McColloch and Cummings.

5. Until the 1970s, batch-processing was the predominant method in data-processing installations. Data would be collected in groups, or batches, and processed at periodic intervals. In this environment the data-processing shop was usually centralized within the corporate structure, and requests would flow from operating departments directly to the data-processing center. When a standard request, for, say, a sales report, came into the department, it would be sent directly to the operations set-up crew, usually called input/output control section. They would check the request to see that it met previously established standards and set-up control statements for processing. The work would then be forwarded to the machine room where operators would run the job. After processing, the results would be routed back to the input/output control section, where the output would be checked, and

appropriate control totals posted in a log book. Once the reports were checked they would be sent back to the requesting department.

6. For an explanation and analysis of the emerging forms of management organization, see Maarten de Kadt, "The Development of Management Structures: the Problem of the Control of Workers in Large Corporations" (Ph.D. dissertation New School for Social Research, 1976).

7. See Philip Kraft, *Managers and Programmers* (New York: Springer-Verlag, 1977), pp. 37–38.

8. Samuel I. Doctors, *The Role of Federal Agencies in Technology Transfer* (Cambridge: MIT Press, 1969), Preface.

9. Ibid.

10. U.S. v. IBM, begun in 1969, is possible one of the biggest trials in U.S. history. The mountains of evidence introduced by IBM fill file cabinets along an entire wall in the mammoth courtroom. The government's antitrust legal staff is camped between boxes of documents, which take up many offices. To date hundreds of thousands of documents have been entered into evidence. Clearly, the length and scope of the trial are beyond any quick summary as well as beyond the focus of this study. I am extremely grateful to Catherine Arnst, who covered the trial for *Computerworld*, for filling me in on the major events. The items I have selected to discuss here were gleaned from discussions with her; *Computerworld* reports on the trial; my brief visits to the trial; and a major document entered as evidence against IBM called "IBM Confidential: Memo to Mr. F. T. Cary, draft from Hilary Faw, 12/10/71" which describes IBM's pricing strategies. IBM tried to keep this particular memo out of the trial, fighting its introduction as evidence all the way to the Supreme Court, but was unsuccessful.

11. Testimony by Dr. Alan McAdams, U.S. v. IBM, trial, July 8, 1977.

12. Ibid.

13. Evidence presented at U.S. v. IBM trial, entitled "IBM Confidential: Memo to Mr. F. T. Carey, draft from Hilary Faw 12/10/71" (emphasis in original).

14. Ibid., emphasis in original.

15. Ibid.

16. Faw's arguments concern "systems programmers," who are, by most accounts, the most technically skilled among data-processing workers. As other data-processing jobs become increasingly deskilled, it is the systems programmers (hotshots or honchos) who pick up the technical pieces. Emphasis added.

Chapter 8

1. Gerald M. Weinberg, *The Psychology of Computer Programming* (New York: Van Nostrand Reinhold, 1971), especially Part II, "Programming as a Social Activity;" and Philip Kraft, *Programmers and Managers* (New York: Springer-Verlag, 1977).

2. I don't pretend to be a psychologist or even a practicing sociologist. The attempt here is to capture some of the flavor of workplace customs and depict the influence this has on work organization. It is based mostly on my own experiences in the field, the in-depth interviews conducted for this study, and information I have collected as data-processing instructor. Although these data cannot be considered statistically sound in terms of being drawn from accurate samples, they do nevertheless reflect generally acknowledged tendencies among data-processing workers and correspond to the growing body of literature about workers and work today.

3. Report of a Special Task Force to the Secretary of Health, Education, and Welfare, *Work in America* (Cambridge: MIT Press, 1973). In particular see chaps. 1, 2.

4. Ibid., p. 13.

5. See Richard Sennet and Jonathan Cobb, *The Hidden Injuries of Class* (New York: Vintage Books, 1973). They describe this process for blue-collar workers; see in particular, Part II, "Dreams and Defenses."

6. Milt Stone, "The Quality of Life," *Datamation*, 18, no. 2 (February 1972), p. 40.

7. "A Profile of the Programmer," a study by Deutch and Shea, Inc., (New York: Industrial Relations News, 1963).

8. See Sennett and Cobb, especially Chap. 4. Their study illustrates the ways workers adapt their aspirations to the definition of the job.

9. LaGuardia Community College is a work-study school, where students alternate terms in the classroom with terms on a full-time job. The questionnaire is given to students, according to major fields, before they go on their first work internships. It is also routinely administered when they return. I used the job characteristics from the questionnaire to follow up on students after graduation. See also Jeremy Brecher and Tim Costello, *Common Sense For Hard Times* (New York: Two Continents Press; Washington, D.C.: Institute for Policy Studies, 1976), for moving descriptions about interests and aspirations of workers.

10. *Work in America*, p. 39.

11. See Ivar Berg, with Sherry Gorelick, *Education and Jobs: The Great Training Robbery* (New York: Frederick Praeger, 1970).

12. Reported in *Computerworld*, March 3, 1977, p. 15.

13. Andrew Friedman, *Industry and Labour, Class Struggle at Work and Monopoly Capitalism* (London: Macmillan, 1977), p. 53.

14. See Chap. 5 for analysis of performance evaluation through trait-rating.

15. Mobility outside the department is also blocked. Most companies have their established paths to top management, and data-processing workers agree that their department is not a route on that path. Usually the older, more established departments, Marketing or Finance, for instance, are more accepted into upper management.

16. There is a possibly apocryphal story that a group of operators were physically locked in the machine room during the 1977 New York power

blackout. Many companies are using electronic passcard systems to keep workers out of or in certain areas.

17. See Kraft, Chap. 4, for an excellent description of the physical environs of programmers.

18. There are two types of terminals: printer devices, which like standard typewriters can make a lot of noise; and CRT's, which are quieter, although recent evidence points out that these "tubes" are terrible for eyesight, causing severe headaches.

19. Reported in *Computerworld*, June 13, 1977, p. 1.

20. "A Profile of the Programmer," pp. 47–49.

21. A. P. Ershov, "Aesthetics and the Human Factor in Programming," *Communications of the ACM* 15, no. 7 (July 1972), p. 503.

22. See Studs Terkel, *Working* (New York: Avon Books, 1975), for a collection of interviews with workers outlining their frustrations and visions.

23. Sennett and Cobb, p. 22.

24. See Weinberg for some interesting stories about programmer pranks and the importance of the informal networks that develop from these relationships.

25. *Computerworld*, December 20, 1976, p. 1.

26. Ibid., July 4, 1977, p. 1.

27. The issue of computer crime and its prevention is a regular topic in most trade publications and at data-processing conferences. It is discussed so extensively one wonders that all computer centers and data-processing workers are not permanently sealed in airtight compartments. To judge from the management literature on the issue, drastic measures are not far away.

28. Weinberg, pp. 78–79, relates a classic "working-to-rule" case. He describes the situation in which a manager requires programmers to work the regular company hours. They do so, but of course no work gets done since the programmers' "real" work day had always occurred after hours, when they could get the machine-time they needed to test their programs. I've seen this kind of thing happen many times.

Another equally common work rule concerns filling out time sheets that detail the tasks done by the programmers each day. Frustrated programmers may simply spend more time filling out their time sheets than working!

29. Before the days of online terminals, program listings and/or card decks found their way into the waste basket. Now, since these vital elements are kept on disk, the method used is to "erase" their image from the program library by mistake.

30. Weinberg, p. 61.

31. See Kenneth Rau, "Improved Productivity of the Computer Resource," paper presented at a National Conference on Computer Systems Productivity, Washington, D.C., June 28, 1977. Rau differentiates as many managers do, efficiency and effectiveness of systems. *Efficiency* addresses "how much of a resource is consumed," and *effectiveness* explores "how well the objectives are being accomplished."

Chapter 9

1. *Computerworld,* August 8, 1977, p. 1.
2. *Wall Street Journal,* May 12, 1977, p. 40.
3. Karl Marx, *Capital,* Vol. I (New York: International Publishers, 1974), p. 363.
4. The point that management ideology uses efficiency as a mask for social control is painfully illustrated in the example of the Soviet Union. Lenin borrowed freely from Frederick Taylor's Scientific Management, and today's systems are heavily endowed with formulas from Western management science. If real change is to take place, this example should help us realize that the social relations—the way we relate to one another—must change. For this to happen we must pay close attention to how pervasive management science is in reinforcing current social relations.

Bibliography

Aitken, Hugh G. J. *Taylorism at the Watertown Arsenal, Scientific Management in Action 1905–1919*. Cambridge: Harvard University Press, 1960.

Argyris, Chris. *Integrating the Individual and the Organization*. New York: John Wiley and Sons, 1964.

Aronowitz, Stanley. "Marx, Technology and Labor." Ph.D. dissertation, Union Graduate School, 1975.

Baker, F. F. "Chief Programmer Team Management of Production Programming." *IBM Systems Journal* 11, 1972, pp. 56–73.

Becker, Gary S. *Human Capital; A Theoretical and Empirical Analysis, with Special Reference to Education*. 2d ed. New York: National Bureau of Economic Research, Columbia University Press, 1975.

Bell, Daniel. *The Cultural Contradictions of Capitalism*. New York: Basic Books, 1976.

———. *Work and its Discontents, The Cult of Efficiency in America*. Boston: Beacon Press, 1956.

Bendix, Reinhard. *Work and Authority in Industry*. Berkeley and Los Angeles: University of California Press, 1956, 1974.

Berg, Ivar, with Sherry Gorelick. *Education and Jobs: The Great Training Robbery*. New York: Frederick A. Praeger, 1970.

Blau, Peter M. *The Dynamics of Bureaucracy*. Chicago: University of Chicago Press, 1963.

———. "The Hierarchy of Authority in Organizations." *American Journal of Sociology* 73, January 1968, pp. 453–467.

———and Marshall Meyer. *Bureaucracy and Modern Society*. 2d ed. New York: Random House, 1971.

Blum, Albert A. "White Collar Workers." In Irene Traviss, ed. *The Computer Impact*. Englewood Cliffs, N.J.: Prentice-Hall, 1970.

Boguslaw, Robert. *The New Utopians: A Study of Systems Design and Social Change.* Englewood Cliffs, N.J.: Prentice-Hall, 1965.

Boore, William F. and Jerry R. Murphy, eds. *The Computer Sampler: Management Perspectives on the Computer.* New York: McGraw-Hill, 1968.

Bowles, Samuel, and Herbert Gintis. *Schooling in Capitalist America, Educational Reform and the Contradictions of Economic Life.* New York: Basic Books, 1976.

Brandon, Dick H. "The Economics of Computer Programming." In George F. Weinwurm, ed. *On the Management of Computer Programming.* Philadelphia: Auerbach Publishers, 1970.

――――. *Management Planning for Data Processing.* New York: Brandon System Press, 1970.

――――. *Management Standards for Data Processing.* New York: Van Nostrand, 1963.

―――― and Fredrich Kirch. "The Case for DP Standards." *Computers and Automation,* 12, November 1963, pp. 28–31.

Braverman, Harry. *Labor and Monopoly Capital, The Degradation of Work in the Twentieth Century.* New York: Monthly Review Press, 1975.

Brecher, Jeremy, and Tim Costello. *Common Sense for Hard Times.* New York: Two Continents Press; Washington, D.C.: Institute for Policy Studies, 1976.

Bright, James R. *Automation and Management.* Cambridge: Harvard University Press, 1958.

Brock, Gerald W. *The U.S. Computer Industry, A Study of Market Power.* Cambridge, Mass.: Ballinger Publishing Co., 1975.

Brooks, Frederick P., Jr. *The Mythical Man-Month, Essays on Software Engineering.* Reading, Mass.: Addison-Wesley, 1975.

Bukharin, N. I., et al. *Science at the Crossroads.* Papers from the Second International Congress of the History of Science and Technology 1931. 2d ed. London: Frank Cass and Co., 1971.

Burton, John F., Jr., et al., eds. *Readings in Labor Market Analysis.* New York: Holt, Rinehart, and Winston, 1971.

Canning, Robert J., and Roger L. Sisson. *The Management of Data Processing.* New York: John Wiley and Sons, 1967.

Chandler, Alfred D., Jr. *Strategy and Structure: Chapters in the History of American Industrial Enterprise.* Cambridge: MIT Press, 1962.

Churchman, C. West. *The Systems Approach.* New York: Delacorte Press, 1968.

Couger, Daniel, *"Pitfalls and Potentials for EDP Training."* Data Management 12, November 1974.

Cummings, Laird. "Rationalization and Automation of Clerical Work." Masters Thesis, Brooklyn College, School of Sociology, 1977.

―――― and Joan Greenbaum. "The Struggle over Productivity: Workers, Management and Technology." In *U.S. Capitalism in Crisis,* Union for Radical Political Economics, January 1978, pp. 55–62.

Dale, Ernest. *Management: Theory and Practice.* 3d ed. New York: McGraw-Hill, 1973.

de Kadt, Maarten. "The Development of Management Structures: The Problem of the Control of Workers in Large Corporations." Ph.D. dissertation, New School for Social Research, Economics 1976.

————. "The Importance of Distinguishing Between Levels of Generality." *Review of Radical Political Economics* 8, Fall 1976, pp. 65–67.

DeMaagd, Gerald R. "Matrix Management." *Datamation* 16, pp. 46–49.

Deutsch and Shea, Inc. "A Profile of the Programmer." New York: Industrial Relations News, 1963. Now Deutsch, Shea and Evans, Inc., 49 E. 53rd St., New York.

Doctors, Samuel I. *The Role of Federal Agencies in Technology Transfer.* Cambridge: MIT Press, 1969.

Doeringer, Peter B., and Michael J. Piore. *Internal Labor Markets and Manpower Analysis.* Lexington, Mass.: Heath Lexington Books, 1971.

Dolotta, T. A., M. I. Bernstein, R. S. Dickson, Jr., N. A. France, B. A. Rosenblatt, D. P. Smith, and T. B. Steel, Jr. *Data Processing in 1980–85: A Study of Potential Limitations to Progress.* New York: John Wiley and Sons, 1976.

Dowling, William F., and Leonard R. Sayles. *How Managers Motivate: The Imperatives of Supervision.* New York: McGraw-Hill, 1971.

Drucker, Peter F. *The Age of Discontinuity.* New York: Harper and Row, 1969.

————. *Management: Tasks, Responsibilities, Practices.* New York: Harper and Row, 1974.

————. *The Practice of Management.* New York: Harper and Row, 1954.

————. *Technology, Management, and Society.* New York: Harper and Row, 1970.

Edwards, Richard C. "Alienation and Inequality: Capitalist Relations of Production in Bureaucratic Enterprise." Ph.D. dissertation, Harvard University, 1972.

————. "The Social Relations of Production in the Firm and Labor Market Structure." In Richard C. Edwards, Michael Reich, David M. Gordon, eds. *Labor Market Segmentation.* Lexington, Mass.: D. C. Heath, 1975.

Ershov, A. P. "Aesthetics and the Human Factor in Programming." *Communications of the ACM* 15, July 1972, pp. 501–505.

Friedman, Andrew L. *Industry and Labour, Class Struggle at Work and Monopoly Capitalism.* London: MacMillan 1977.

Gagne, Robert M., ed. *Psychological Principles in System Development.* New York: Holt, Rinehart, and Winston, 1962.

Gerth, H. H., and C. Wright Mills. *From Max Weber: Essays in Sociology.* New York: Oxford University Press, 1946.

Gilchrist, Bruce, and Richard E. Weber. "Employment of Trained Computer Personnel—A Quantitative Survey." *Spring Joint Computer Conference Proceedings, 1972*. Montvale, N.J.: AFIPS Press, 1972.

———. "Sources of Trained Computer Personnel—a Quantitative Survey." *Spring Joint Computer Conference Proceedings, 1972*. Montvale, N.J.: AFIPS Press, 1972.

Gildersleeve, Thomas R. *Data Processing Project Management*. New York: Van Nostrand Reinhold, 1974.

Gintis, Herbert. "The Nature of Labor Exchange and the Theory of Capitalist Production." *Review of Radical Political Economics* 8, Summer 1976, pp. 36–54.

Glenn, Evelyn Nakano, and Roslyn L. Feldberg. "Degraded and Deskilled: The Proletarianization of Clerical Work." *Social Problems* 25, October 1977, pp. 52–64.

Goldstine, Herman H. *The Computer from Pascal to Von Neuman*. Princeton: Princeton University Press, 1972.

Gordon, David M. "Capitalist Efficiency and Socialist Efficiency." *Monthly Review* 28, July-August 1976, pp. 19–39.

Greenbaum, Joan. "Automation, A Look at the Basic Assumptions." *Computers and Society,* Fall 1975, pp. 4–5.

———. "Division of Labor in the Computer Field." *Monthly Review* 28, July-August 1976, pp. 40–55.

——— and Meryl L. Sussman. "A Model for Integration of Cooperative Education and the Classroom." *Journal of Cooperative Education* 12, May 1976, pp. 66–76.

Hales, Mike. "Management Science and the Second Industrial Revolution." *Radical Science Journal* 1, January 1974, pp. 3–28.

Hall, Richard H. *Occupations and Social Structure*. Englewood Cliffs, N.J.: Prentice-Hall, 1975.

Hamblen, John W., "Production and Utilization of Computer Manpower in the U.S." *Spring Joint Computer Conference Proceedings, Communications of the ACM*. Montvale, N.J.: AFIPS Press.

Harvard Business Review: On Management. New York: Harper and Row, 1975.

Hickson, David, and D. S. Pugh, Diana C. Pheysey. "Operations, Technology and Organization Structure." *Administrative Science Quarterly* 14, September 1969, pp. 378–397.

Hoberman, Robert S. "Lowering Programmer Turnover Rates." *Infosystems* 23, May 1976.

Hoos, Ida. *Automation in the Office*. Washington, D.C.: Public Affairs Press, 1961.

Horowitz, Ira. *Decision Making and the Theory of the Firm*. New York: Holt, Rinehart, and Winston, 1970.

Institute of Life Insurance. *Life Insurance Fact Book*. New York. Annual

Kast, Fremont E., and James E. Rosenzweig. *Organization and*

Management: A Systems Approach. 2d ed. New York: McGraw-Hill, 1974.

Kauffman, Carl B. *Man Incorporate, The Individual and His Work in An Organized Society.* Garden City, N.Y.: Doubleday 1967.

Koontz, Harold, and Cyril O. O'Donnell. *Principles of Management: An Analysis of Managerial Functions.* New York: McGraw-Hill, 1972

Kraft, Philip. *Programmers and Managers, The Routinization of Computer Programming in the United States.* New York: Heidelberg Science Library; Springer-Verlag, 1977.

Lecht, Charles. *The Management of Computer Programming Projects.* New York: American Management Association, Inc. 1967.

———. *Waves of Change.* New York: Advanced Computer Techniques Inc., 1977.

Leibenstein, Harvey. "Allocative Efficiency vs X-Efficiency." *American Economic Review* 56, June 1966, pp. 392–415.

Likert, Rensis. *The Human Organization.* New York: McGraw-Hill, 1967.

Litwak, Eugene. "Technological Innovation and Theoretical Functions of Primary Groups and Bureaucratic Structure." *American Journal of Sociology* 74, January 1968, pp. 468–481.

Maccoby, Michael. *The Gamesman. The New Corporate Leaders.* New York: Simon and Schuster, 1976.

Malcolm, D. G., and A. J. Rowe. *Management Control Systems.* New York: John Wiley and Sons, 1960.

March, James, and Herbert Simon. *Organization.* New York: John Wiley and Sons, 1958.

Marglin, Stephen A. "What Do Bosses Do? The Origins and Functions of Hierarchy in Capitalist Production." *Review of Radical Political Economics* 6, Summer 1974, pp. 33–60.

———. "Postscript Notes." unpublished mimeograph, August 1975.

Marx, Karl. *Capital.* Volumes I, II, III. New York: International Publishers, 1974.

———. *A Contribution to the Critique of Political Economy.* New York: International Publishers, 1970.

Maslow, Abraham. *Motivation and Personality.* New York: Harper and Row, 1954.

Mayer, David, and Ashford W. Stalmaker. "Selection of Evaluation of Computer Personnel." In George F. Weinwurm, ed. *On the Management of Computer Programming.* Philadelphia: Auerbach Publishers, 1970.

McColloch, Mark. "White-Collar Electrical Machinery, Banking, and Public Welfare Workers 1940–1970." Ph.D. dissertation, University of Pittsburgh, 1975.

McGregor, Douglas. *The Human Side of Enterprise.* New York: McGraw-Hill, 1960.

———. "Perspectives on Organization and the Manager's Role." In

George P. Schultz and Thomas L. Whisler, eds. *Management Organization and the Computer*. Glencoe, Ill.: Free Press, 1960.

McKinsey and Company. "Getting the Most Out of Your Computer." Report. 1963; "Unlocking the Computer Profit Potential." Report. 1968. New York.

Meyer, Marshall. "Automation and Bureaucratic Structure." *American Journal of Sociology* 74, no. 3, 1968, pp. 256–264.

Mills, C. Wright. *White Collar, The American Middle Class*. London: Oxford University Press, 1951.

Montagna, Paul. *Occupations and Society, Toward a Sociology of the Labor Market*. New York: John Wiley and Sons, 1977.

Myers, Charles A., ed. *The Impact of Computers on Management*. Cambridge: MIT Press, 1967.

Nelson, Edward A. "Some Recent Contributions to Computer Programming Management." In George F. Weinwurm, ed. *On the Management of Computer Programming*. Philadelphia: Auerbach Publishers, 1970.

Noble, F. David. *America By Design: Science, Technology, and the Rise of Corporate Capitalism*. New York: Alfred A. Knopf, 1977.

Nyborg, Philip S., and Pender M. McCarter, William Erickson, eds. *Information Processing in the United States, A Quantitative Survey*. Montvale, N.J.: AFIPS Press, 1977.

Palmer, Bryan. "Class, Conception, and Conflict: The Thrust for Efficiency, Managerial Views of Labor, and the Working Class Rebellion 1903–1922." *Review of Radical Political Economics* 7, no. 2, 1975, pp. 31–49.

Patrick, R. L. "Ten Years of Progress?" *Datamation* 14, September 1967, pp. 22–24.

Perry, Dallis, and William Cannon. "Vocational Interests of Computer Programmers." *Journal of Applied Psychology* 51, February 67, pp. 28–34.

———. "Vocational Interests of Female Programmers. *Journal of Applied Psychology* 52, February 1968, pp. 31–35.

Pettigrew, Andrew M. "Occupational Specialization as an Emergent Process." *The Sociological Review* 21, May 1973, pp. 255–278.

Pietrasanta, Alfred M. "Resource Analysis of Computer Program System Development." In George F. Weinwurm, ed. *On the Management of Computer Programming*. Philadelphia: Auerbach Publishers, 1970.

———. "Two Empirical Studies of Program Production." *IFIPS Proceedings* 1968. Montvale, N.J.: AFIPS Press, 1968.

Pigors, Paul, and Charles A. Myers. *Personnel Administration; A Point of View and a Method*. New York: McGraw-Hill, 1976.

Piore, Michael J. "Notes for a Theory of Labor Market Stratification." In Richard C. Edwards, Michael Reich, David M. Gordon, eds. *Labor Market Segmentation*. Lexington, Mass.: D. C. Heath, 1975.

Reich, Michael, and David M. Gordon, Richard C. Edwards. "A Theory of Labor Market Segmentation." *American Economic Review* 63,

May 1973, pp. 359–365.

Reynolds, Carl H. "Program Control." *Datamation*, October 15, 1970.

———. "What's Wrong with Computer Programming Management." In George F. Weinwurm, ed. *On the Management of Computer Programming*. Philadelphia: Auerbach Publishers, 1970.

Reynolds, Lloyd G. *Labor Economics and Labor Relations*. 6th ed. Englewood Cliffs, N.J.: Prentice-Hall, 1974.

Rogers, James, and Donald Bullock. "The Application of Programmed Instruction in the Computer Field." *Computers and Automation*. 12, April 1963, pp. 22–25.

Rosenberg, Nathan. "Marx as a Student of Technology." *Monthly Review* 28, July-August 1976, pp. 56–77.

Rothman, Stanley, and Charles Mosmann. *Computers and Society*. 2d ed. Chicago: SRA, 1976.

Sammet, Jean E. *"Programming Languages: History and Fundamentals*. Englewood Cliffs, N.J.: Prentice-Hall, 1969.

Schultz, George P., and Thomas L. Whisler, eds. *Management Organization and the Computer*. Glencoe, Ill.: Free Press, 1960.

Sennett, Richard, and Jonathan Cobb. *The Hidden Injuries of Class*. New York: Vintage Books, Random House, 1973.

Shapiro, Nina. "The Neoclassical Theory of the Firm." *Review of Radical Political Economics* 8, Winter 1976, pp. 17–29.

Shepard, Jon. *Automation and Alienation, A Study of Office and Factory Workers*. Cambridge: MIT Press, 1971.

Silvern, Gloria M. "Programmed Instruction for Computer Programming." *Computers and Automation* 12, March 1963, pp. 12–18.

Simon, Herbert A. "Management and Decision-Making." In Irene Taviss, ed. *The Computer Impact*. Englewood Cliffs: N.J.: Prentice-Hall, 1970.

———. *The Shape of Automation for Men and Management*. New York: Harper and Row, Torchbooks, 1965.

——— and Allen Newell. "What have Computers to Do with Management." In George P. Schultz and Thomas L. Whisler, eds. *Management Organization and the Computer*. Glencoe, Ill.: Free Press, 1960.

Squire, Enid. *The Computer: An Everyday Machine*. 2d ed. Menlo Park, Calif.: Addison-Wesley, 1977.

Stone, Katherine. "The Origins of Job Structures in the Steel Industry." *Review of Radical Political Economics* 6, no. 2, Summer 1974, pp. 61–97.

Stone, Milt. "The Quality of Life." *Datamation* 18, February 1972, pp. 40–44.

Taviss, Irene. *The Computer Impact*. Englewood Cliffs, N.J.: Prentice-Hall, 1970.

Taylor, Frederick W. "Shop Management." In *Scientific Management*. New York: Harper and Row, 1947.

Terkel Studs. *Working*. New York: Avon Books, 1975.

Tomeski, Edward A. *The Computer Revolution: The Executive and the New Information Technology.* New York: Macmillan, 1970.

U.S. Department of Commerce. Bureau of the Census. *Statistical Abstract of the United States.* Annual.

U.S. Department of Health, Education, and Welfare. *Work in America.* Cambridge: MIT Press, 1973.

U.S. Department of Labor. Bureau of Labor Statistics. *Computer Manpower Outlook.* Bulletin 1826, 1974.

U.S. Department of Labor. Bureau of Labor Statistics. *National Survey of Professional, Administrative, Technical and Clerical Pay.* 1976.

U.S. Department of Labor. Bureau of Labor Statistics. *Occupational Outlook Handbook.* 1970–71 edition. 1974–75 edition. 1976–77 edition.

U.S. Department of Labor. Bureau of Labor Statistics. *Studies of Automatic Technology.* No. 2, "The Introduction of an Electronic Computer in a Large Insurance Company." October 1955.

Wagner, L. G. "Computers, Decentralization and Corporate Control." In William F. Boore and Jerry R. Murphy, eds. *The Computer Sampler.* New York: McGraw-Hill, 1968.

Weber, Richard E., and Bruce Gilchrist. "Discrimination in the Employment of Women in the Computer Industry." *Communications of the ACM* 18, July 1975, pp. 416–418.

Weinburg, Gerald. *The Psychology of Computer Programming.* New York: Van Nostrand Reinhold, 1971.

Weinwurm, George F. "The Challenge to the Management Community" and "On the Economic Analysis of Computer Programming." In George F. Weinwurm, ed. *On The Management of Computer Programming.* Philadelphia: Auerbach Publishers, 1970.

Weizenbaum, Joseph. *Computer Power and Human Reason.* New York: W. H. Freeman, 1976.

Westin, Alan F., and Michael A. Baker. *Databanks in a Free Society, Computers, Record-keeping and Privacy.* Report of the Project on Computer Databanks of the Computer Science and Engineering Board. National Academy of Sciences. New York: Quadrangle Books, 1972.

Whisler, Thomas L. "The Impact of Information Technology on Organizational Control." In Charles A. Myers, ed. *The Impact of Computers on Management.* Cambridge: MIT Press, 1967.

Wiener, Norbert. *The Human Use of Human Beings.* New York: Avon Books, 1967.

Young, Bob. "Science is Social Relations." *Radical Science Journal,* no. 5, pp. 65–118.

Zimbalist, Andrew. "The Limits of Work Humanization." *Review of Radical Political Economics* 7, Summer 1975, pp. 50–59.

USEFUL ADDRESSES

Data-processing Periodicals

Computers and People (formerly *Computers and Automation*). Berkeley Enterprises, Inc., 815 Washington St., Newtonville, Mass. 02160; monthly.

Computerworld, 797 Washington St., Newton, Mass. 02160; weekly.

Data Management, 505 Busse Highway, Park Ridge, Ill. 60068; monthly.

Datamation, Technical Publishing Co., 35 Mason St., Greenwich, Conn., 06830; monthly.

Infosystems (formerly *Business Automation*), Hitchcock Publishing Co., Hitchcock Building, Wheaton, Ill. 60187; monthly.

Journal of Data Processing Education, P.O. Box 867, Soquel, Calif. 95075; quarterly.

Data-processing Associations

American Federation of Information Processing Societies (AIPS), 210 Summit Ave., Montvale, N.J. 07645; proceedings, and AFIPS Press publications.

Association for Educational Data Systems, 1201 16th St., N.W., Washington, D.C. 20036, *The Monitor;* monthly; *Journal;* quarterly.

Association of Computer Programmers and Analysts (ACPA), P.O. Box 95, Kensington, Md., 20795; *Thruput*; monthly; proceedings; annual.

Association of Computing Machinery (ACM), 1133 Avenue of the Americas, N.Y., N.Y., 10036; *Communications of the ACM,* monthly; *Computing Reviews,* monthly; proceedings, publications and newsletters of special interest groups.

Data Processing Management Association (DPMA), 505 Busse Highway, Park Ridge, Ill., 60068; *Data Management;* monthly.

Institute for Certification of Computer Professionals, 304 East 45th St., New York, N.Y. 10017.

International Federation of Information Processing, 3 Rue Du Marche, Geneva 1204, Switzerland; proceedings, publications.

Society of Certified Data Processors, 2670 Union Extended, Suite 532, Memphis, Tennessee, 38112; *Inner Voice*; monthly.

Index

Aiken, Hugh, 36
American Association of Computing Machinery (ACM), 85, 96
Association of Computer Programmers and Analysts, 103
Atanasoff, John, 173
AT&T (American Telegraph and Telephone), 66
AUTOCODER (programming language), 80

Baker, Michael, 14
Batch-processing, 30, 72, 131, 189
Bell Telephone laboratories, 27
Bendix, Reinhard, 59
Benson, Miles, 104–107
Berg, Ivar, 5, 144
Blau, Peter, 114–115, 187
Bowles, Samuel, 49
Brandon, Dick, 16, 63, 88, 187
Braverman, Harry, 8, 47, 49
Brecher, Jeremy, 50, 52, 97, 109
Brooks, Frederick P., Jr., 31, 121–122
Bureaucracy: and authority, 114–115; and behavior, 107;

and motivation, 97; and organization structure, 110–115, 161; worker reaction to, 151–156. *See also* Control; Hierarchy; Management science; Matrix management

Cary, Frank, 134
Census Bureau (U.S.), 13, 26
Central Processing Unit (CPU), 25. *See also* Computer hardware
Certificate in Data Processing (CDP), 103
Chandler, Alfred, 40
Chief programmer teams, 121–122, 188. *See also* Programmers
Churchman, C. West, 40
Cobb, Jonathan, 9, 150
COBOL (programming language), 79. *See also* Operating systems; Systems software
Communications Workers of America (CWA), 103
Computer-aided-instruction, 93, 185

205